AQA

GCSE English Language for post-16

A one-year course

Jo Heathcote

William Collins' dream of knowledge for all began with the publication of his first book in 1819. A self-educated mill worker, he not only enriched millions of lives, but also founded a flourishing publishing house. Today, staying true to this spirit, Collins books are packed with inspiration, innovation and practical expertise. They place you at the centre of a world of possibility and give you exactly what you need to explore it.

Collins. Freedom to teach

HarperCollins Publishers
1 London Bridge Street
London SE1 9GF

10 9 8 7 6 5 4 3 2

ISBN 978-0-00-820933-9

Collins® is a registered trademark of HarperCollins Publishers Limited

www.collins.co.uk

A catalogue record for this book is available from the British Library

Commissioning editor: Catherine Martin
Project managers: Judith Walters and Lesley Gray
Development editors: Judith Walters and Lesley Gray
Project editor: Alexander Rutherford
Editorial project manager: Catherine Dakin
Copyeditor: Catherine Dakin
Proofreader: Claire Throp
Designer: Ken Vail
Typesetter: QBS Learning
Illustrations: QBS Learning
Cover designer: ink-tank and associates
Printer: Grafica Veneta S.p.A. in Italy

With thanks to contributing author Mike Gould for the reuse of material from the AQA GCSE English Language and English Literature: Core Student Book and Advanced Student Book.

With thanks to students and teachers at the following schools and colleges for their help with the project: The Manchester College, Manchester; Peterborough Regional College, Peterborough; Milton Keynes College, Milton Keynes; Barking and Dagenham College, Romford; Joseph Chamberlain Sixth Form College, Birmingham; Northampton School for Girls, Northampton; St Ninian's High School, Isle of Man.

Student Book Introduction

Welcome to your post-16 English course

This textbook is designed to equip you with all of the skills you need for success in AQA GCSE English Language. It is a complete one-year course, helpfully organised into 30 weeks to match your college year.

To keep life simple, the course covers everything you need to tackle for Paper 1 in Term 1 and everything you need to tackle for Paper 2 in Term 2. At the end of the course, in Term 3, you will find mock examination papers to help you practise all of your skills right before the real examination so you will feel fully prepared.

As you work through the book, you will have lots of chances to practise the skills you need for each question. The logical order of this textbook should help you to feel confident in understanding what to do for each question in the final exam. There are practice questions to do every step of the way and helpful checklists to keep everything clear in your mind as you progress.

You will have the chance to read many different extracts from modern short stories and novels in preparation for Paper 1 and a whole variety of non-fiction texts for Paper 2. This means facing unseen texts in the real exam will be something you can do with confidence.

How the book is structured

The book is organised into three terms, just like an academic year. Instead of being structured in chapters, this book gives you two clear lessons for each week of your course.

In **Term 1**, you will begin with some very basic comprehension and reading skills, working with extracts from novels and short stories.

Once you have understood those principles, you will move on to do some creative writing of your own and you will undertake a creative task to measure your progress.

After half term, you will learn how to analyse the language and structure of creative texts. Doing some descriptive writing of your own will help you to use this understanding in Section B of the examination, which tests writing.

Towards the end of Term 1, you will pull all of your skills together by learning how to write longer responses to reading texts and you will have a full mock examination paper to check how you are doing.

In **Term 2** you will prepare for Paper 2 by recapping on your comprehension skills and learning how to tackle 19th century texts. Paper 2 is all about points of view and you will add to your skills set here by preparing for your Spoken Language Endorsement. This Endorsement is a great addition to your CV, showing universities and employers your spoken communication ability. This is also used to prepare you for writing about your point of view more formally for Section B of the final Paper 2 exam.

A little more technical work will build your confidence in dealing with the language of non-fiction texts and, finally, the textbook will pull all of your skills together to show you how to compare texts effectively.

There's a Paper 2 to practise all of your skills and to help you to revise before you tackle those final mock papers in **Term 3** at the very end of your GCSE English Language learning journey.

Contents

What do I need to know?

The Assessment Objectives

The Assessment Objectives give a framework of the skills that you need to show in order to pass the examination and achieve the qualification. They are separated out into three key areas:

- Reading

- Writing

- Spoken language

The assessment objectives are referred to as AOs. You can refer back to the AOs as you progress through the course to check that you understand exactly what skills the examiner is expecting you to show. Use the third column to help you do this.

Reading	What they say	What they mean for you
AO1	Identify and interpret explicit and implicit information and ideas. Select and synthesise evidence from different texts.	At the end of your course you need to be able to show that you can • read carefully and with understanding • pick out the right types of information when asked (the explicit information) • show your understanding of what you read by being able to back up your thoughts with evidence • make suggestions about what things might mean or suggest to you (the implicit information) • read well enough to be able to draw together information from more than one text at once (synthesising).
AO2	Explain, comment on and analyse how writers use language and structure to achieve effects and influence readers, using relevant subject terminology to support their views.	At the end of your course in English Language you need to • have some knowledge about the language you've studied and be able to 'put it under a microscope' and examine it in close-up • be able to think about why language is used in certain ways and how it might make you think and feel • look at the ways pieces of writing are put together to make a particular impression on you.
AO3	Compare writers' ideas and perspectives, as well as how these are conveyed, across two or more texts.	You need to be able to show that • you can read different texts – some of them more challenging than others – and be able to decide what they are about and what their main ideas are • you can understand what the people writing were trying to say and what their different points of view are • you can compare the similar or different viewpoints in two texts • you can compare the language and structure used in both texts.

Reading	What they say	What they mean for you
AO4	Evaluate texts critically and support this with appropriate textual references.	At the end of your course you need to • show you are a thoughtful reader, so that when you read things you can weigh up what is being written and think about the message it may be giving you • be able to understand the meaning of what you read but also what the writer was doing to make you see that meaning • think about putting the language under the microscope again to consider how the things you read are put together (this will also be really useful in helping you become a better writer) • show your understanding by being able to back up your thoughts and ideas with evidence.
AO5	Communicate clearly, effectively and imaginatively, selecting and adapting tone, style and register for different forms, purposes and audiences. Organise information and ideas, using structural and grammatical features to support coherence and cohesion of texts.	You need to show that • you can write well and communicate clearly, no matter who it is you're writing for • you can write in different ways to be able to be a good all-round communicator • you are able to build and organise your writing so that it makes sense, but also so that it does what you want it to do (achieve your purpose).
AO6	Candidates must use a range of vocabulary and sentence structures for clarity, purpose and effect, with accurate spelling and punctuation. (This requirement must constitute 20% of the marks for each specification as a whole.)	You need your writing to show that • you can use the English language well • you have a good vocabulary • you can spell and punctuate your work in a way that shows you are clear and accurate.
AO7	Demonstrate presentation skills in a formal setting.	You need to show that you can • speak using the English language in a way that is not just chatty and friendly, but precise and convincing when presenting your views and ideas • give a presentation to other people in this style.
AO8	Listen and respond appropriately to spoken language, including questions and feedback on presentations.	When other people are speaking, you can • listen • respond • and reply. If they are presenting to you, you need to show that you • are a thoughtful listener • pay attention to what they have said • can ask helpful questions about it.
AO9	Use spoken Standard English effectively in speeches and presentations.	When it is needed, you can speak in a way that is clear and understandable to everyone as well as being polite. You can speak in public using your best English and avoiding slang or words from your own dialect that others may not understand.

The Question Papers

To pass your AQA GCSE English Language, you will need to complete two examinations and give a formal spoken presentation to achieve your Spoken language endorsement.

Paper 1 is called 'Explorations in creative reading and writing.'

Paper 2 is called 'Writers' viewpoints and perspectives'.

Paper 1: Explorations in creative reading and writing

In this paper, you will be given a passage to read from a short story or a novel. It will have a modern feel and will have been written in either the 20th or 21st century.

You will be asked to complete four questions on the passage. You will then be asked to complete a piece of creative writing on a topic linked to the passage.

The first part of the questions will follow a pattern and will test the Assessment Objectives in order.

AO1: 4 marks	**1.** List four things…
AO2: 8 marks	**2.** How does the writer's use of language…
AO2: 8 marks	**3.** How does the writer structure…
AO4: 20 marks	**4.** To what extent do you agree…
AO5: 24 marks and AO6: 16 marks	**5.** Write a narrative about… and/or write a description of…

Paper 2: Writers' viewpoints and perspectives

In this paper you will be given two passages to read, with a connecting theme or idea. One of these passages will be from the 19th century (1800–1899). This will mean the style and language may not be so familiar and will be a little more challenging.

Again, you will be asked to complete four questions based on what you have read. You will then be asked to complete a piece of writing presenting your own point of view on a topic linked to the passages.

The first part of the questions will follow a pattern and will test the Assessment Objectives in order.

AO1: 4 marks	1. True/false statements…
AO1: 8 marks	2. Write a summary of…
AO2: 12 marks	3. How does the writer's use of language…
AO3: 16 marks	4. Compare how the writers present…
AO5: 24 marks and AO6: 16 marks	5. Write an (article/speech/letter)… presenting your viewpoint on…

Introducing basic comprehension skills

You are learning to:
- read carefully, picking out the right types of information
- show your understanding by being able to back up your thoughts with evidence.

Testing: AO1
For: Paper 1, Question 1 and building skills for Question 4

1 Getting you thinking

In your day-to-day life, you spend a lot of time reading different texts for information. You also make hundreds of decisions accepting some of this information and rejecting other aspects of it.

 a Think about a typical day. Which of these information sources do you make use of?

- cooking instructions on food packaging
- traffic information
- weather forecast
- name or content labels on sandwiches, snacks or drinks
- records in a homework diary
- a 'to do' list
- text messages from friends

b Think about your day today.

- Make a list of information sources you have come across so far.
- What are the three most important things on your list? Why? How did you decide?

Heating Guidelines

Ensure food is piping hot before serving.
As appliances vary, the following timings are guidelines only.
- **remove from outer packaging and foil tray**
- transfer to a baking tray
- heat in the centre of pre-heated oven

⬚ Conventional Oven		⚙ Fan Oven	
Temp. Mark 6 200°C 400°F	from fresh **20-25** mins	Temp. Mark 5 190°C 375°F	from fresh **20-25** mins
	from frozen **35-40** mins		from frozen **35-40** mins

Caution

Not suitable for people on a low or restricted potassium diet.

---

② Explore the skills

Being able to select the key **factual** information or **explicit meaning** is the first stepping stone to understanding any text you read.

Key terms

factual: information that is true and can be proved

explicit meaning: the basic information on the surface – the true or literal; what is stated directly

a Look at this extract from the opening of a short story, 'The Darkness Out There', in which two young people visit an old lady, Mrs Rutter, to do some odd jobs for her.

> She seemed composed of circles, a cottage-loaf of a woman, with a face below which chins collapsed one into another, a creamy smiling pool of a face in which her eyes snapped and darted.
>
> 'Tea, my duck?' she said. 'Tea for the both of you? I'll put us a kettle on.'
>
> The room was stuffy. It had a gaudy lino floor with the pattern rubbed away in front of the sink and round the table; the walls were cluttered with old calendars and pictures torn from magazines; there was a smell of cabbage. The alcove by the fireplace was filled with china ornaments: big-eyed flop-eared rabbits and beribboned kittens and flowery milkmaids and a pair of naked chubby children wearing daisy chains.
>
> The woman hauled herself from a sagging armchair. She glittered at them from the stove, manoeuvring cups, propping herself against the draining-board. 'What's your names, then? Sandra and Kerry. Well, you're a pretty girl, Sandra, aren't you. Pretty as they come. There was – let me see, who was it? – Susie, last week. That's right, Susie.' Her eyes investigated, quick as mice. 'Put your jacket on the back of the door, dear, you won't want to get that messy. Still at school, are you?'
>
> Penelope Lively, 'The Darkness Out There' from *Pack of Cards*

b Look at this Paper 1, Question 1 examination-style task:

List four things from the extract about the room in Mrs Rutter's cottage.

Now you are going to read to pick out the key information.

Carefully read through the text to pick out as many things as you can about Mrs Rutter's cottage that are **explicitly stated**.

Present your information clearly in either:

- short, crisp sentences
- a bullet-pointed list.

Now look at Student A's response to the task:

> 1. stuffy
> 2. 'the walls were cluttered with old calendars and pictures torn from magazines; there was a smell of'
> 3. The pattern is rubbed away in front of the sink.
> 4. It seems that the room is quite untidy and a bit of a mess.

Student A's response shows some of the most common mistakes that can be made when answering this type of basic question.

Remembering that the focus of the task is 'the room':

- How many of Student A's answers are definitely correct?

- Make some notes on what Student A has done here that makes it difficult for them to score full marks.

d Now look at Student B's response to the task:

> 1. The room had cluttered walls.
> 2. The room has a fireplace.
> 3. The room smells of cabbage.
> 4. It was stuffy.

- How many of Student B's answers are correct?
- What has Student B done here to ensure full marks?

Checklist for success

- Present your response to Question 1 in a numbered list.
- Use short, sharp, clear sentences.
- Use only things that are given to you in the extract and that you can identify as being true.

③ Develop the skills

When you work to build longer comprehension responses for Question 4, you need to be able to back up your selected points with evidence. The evidence takes the form of quotations from the text. Quotations prove that what you are saying is true and accurate.

Exam tip

Think about how you could identify and mark up the information in an exam when you don't have much time.

You could:

- use different colours to highlight information
- underline the information in different styles

- number each example you find.

a Look at these responses that a student has made to this task:

What do you learn about Mrs Rutter from this extract?

> I learn that Mrs Rutter "seemed composed of circles".
> I also learned that she hauled herself from a sagging
> armchair, 'The woman hauled herself from a sagging
> armchair.'

b In the first sentence, can you identify the point that the student is making? Have they used the quotation to support their idea?

c In the second sentence, is it clear what the student has actually understood?

d What do you notice about the way the student has used punctuation to present their quotations?

e Now look at a second student's work in response to the same question and identify the key differences in their approach:

> From the extract we learn that Mrs Rutter is
> rounded in shape as she is described as being
> 'composed of circles, a cottage-loaf of a woman'.
> Mrs Rutter seems alert as 'her eyes snapped
> and darted'.

Begins with a strong, clear statement in the student's own words.

This quotation is genuinely 'embedded' in the sentence as it begins with 'as' and continues to make sense from there.

The student does not waste time copying out a lengthy quotation.

Punctuation to close the sentence is placed after the quotation mark.

4 Final task

a Using the annotations above to help you, write a set of clear instructions for this stronger method of supporting ideas and using quotations. You could begin as follows:
1. Make a strong clear statement in my own words that is directly linked to the question.

b Now practise your skills using your set of instructions.

- List four things from the extract about Mrs Rutter.

- What do you learn about Mrs Rutter's room?

Developing comprehension skills

You are learning to:
- show your understanding by being able to back up your thoughts with evidence
- make suggestions about what things might mean or suggest to you to show your understanding.

Testing: AO1
For: Paper 1 building skills for Question 4

1 Getting you thinking

To really show that you understand a text, you need to able to demonstrate that you can move beyond the **explicit meanings**. This means thinking about the content of the text and showing that you can 'read between the lines'. This is called making **inferences**.

Imagine the conversation below taking place between two friends.

a Is B agreeing or disagreeing with A? Are they being serious or sarcastic? If this is not said explicitly, how do you know? How could you work out B's meaning?

Making inferences or finding **implicit meanings** is a higher-level skill.

Key terms

explicit meanings: the basic information on the surface – the true or literal; what is stated directly

inferences: explanations of what you have been able to read between the lines

implicit meanings: the meanings that you have to work out by reading between the lines; things that are suggested rather than stated

A: What do you think to my new top? Cool or what?

B: It's certainly got short sleeves, mate.

② Explore the skills

Now that you have learned how to identify a key point and used evidence to support it, you can go one step further. You can question yourself about it in order to work out what is suggested or implied. This is how you make your inference.

a Read this extract from the short story 'Your Shoes' by Michèle Roberts.

> I thought I knew you as well as I know this house. No secret places, no hidey-holes, nothing in you I couldn't see. Now I realise how you kept yourself from me, how I didn't really know you at all.
>
> You're not here any longer so how can I speak to you? You can't speak to someone who isn't there. Only mad people talk to an empty chest of drawers, a bed that hasn't been slept in for weeks. Someone half-mad, with grief that is, might pick up a shoe from the rug and hold it like a baby. Someone like me might do that. As if the shoe might still be warm or give a clue to where you've gone.
>
> Michèle Roberts, 'Your Shoes'

b Look at these quotations from the text. Make notes about what is suggested to you by each one. What is implied here that isn't being said explicitly? This will lead you to make some inferences of your own. The first one has been done for you.

Key term

first-person narrator: when a character in a story tells it in their voice using 'I'. This makes it feel like they are sharing their experiences with you

first-person narrator and addressing the story to someone

suggests a secret of some kind or a shock or surprise – sounds disappointed, though

1. 'I thought I knew you as well as I know this house.'

didn't know them as well as she thought

the person she's talking to is familiar to her – maybe lives with her?

2. 'You're not here any longer so how can I speak to you?'

3. 'a bed that hasn't been slept in for weeks.'

4. 'Someone half-mad with grief that is, might pick up a shoe from the rug and hold it like a baby.'

c The narrator of this story is a woman. From the inferences you have made:

- what do you understand about her so far?
- who might the person be, that she is addressing?

③ Develop the skills

a Now go on to read a second extract from the same story. Select four quotations of your own that you feel tell us more about the woman in the story and her feelings.

What did you have for lunch today? I hope you ate something. Did you beg for the money to buy a burger or a sandwich? I'd like to think you had a proper lunch. Something hot. Soup, perhaps, in a Styrofoam cup. You used to love tinned tomato soup. Cream of. I always urged you to eat proper meals, meat and two veg or something salady, when you got home from school. You liked snacks better as you got older, it was the fashion amongst your friends I think, all day long you ate crisps and buns and I don't know what, at teatime when you came in you'd say you weren't hungry then late at night I'd catch you raiding the kitchen cupboards. Fistfuls of currants and sultanas you'd jam into your mouth, one custard cream after another, you'd wolf all my supply of chocolate bars.

b Write out your four quotations and make notes on what is suggested or implied by them.

c How does this now add to your understanding of the woman, the situation she may be in and her feelings about it?

d Have you worked out who is missing, just from your inferences?

Now you are going to put together all of the different elements that show your understanding:

- your ability to **retrieve** key information
- your ability to **support** your idea with evidence
- your ability to demonstrate your understanding with an **inference**.

e Look at the example below and work out what the student has done to cover all three of these skills. Can you identify where they have included each skill?

> The woman in the story is addressing someone with whom she is familiar, as she says, 'I thought I knew you as well as I know this house'. This suggests that the person maybe lived with her and has done something that has come as a shock or surprise to the woman, something out of character for the person she is addressing.

④ Final task

You are now going to use both extracts from the story, your ideas and quotations and the inferences you have made so far from both extracts, to answer this task which builds skills for Paper 1 Question 4:

What is your impression of the woman in the story and how she is feeling?

Write up three ideas using the methods in the **Checklist for success** to show that you really understand the text.

Checklist for success

- Make clear statements in your own words, addressing the question directly.
- Support those statements with your selected quotations.
- Demonstrate your understanding using the inferences you have made.

Applying comprehension skills to Paper 1 Section A

You are learning to:
- read carefully and with understanding, picking out the right types of information
- show your understanding of what you read by being able to back up your thoughts with evidence
- make suggestions about what things might mean or suggest to you to show your understanding.

Testing: AO1
For: Paper 1, Question 1 and building skills for Question 4

1 Getting you thinking

Any piece of creative writing that is the work of an author's imagination is known as a work of **fiction**. Fiction is usually organised into **forms** such as short stories or **novels**.

a   Look at the titles of these novels. Make some notes on what you imagine these works of fiction could be about, just by thinking about the words in each title. What places might they take us to? What kinds of people might we meet in these novels? An example has been done to get you started.

Title	Place	Type of people
The Catcher in the Rye	Tall crop fields stretching into the distance – maybe in America?	'Catcher' suggests someone hiding there, waiting to catch people? Sinister.
Lord of the Flies		
Miss Smilla's Feeling for Snow		
Paddy Clarke Ha Ha Ha		
The Girl Who Played with Fire		
The Wasp Factory		

Key terms

fiction: any type of story that is from the imagination of its writer

forms: categories or types of texts that have similar characteristics

novels: long stories with characters and actions, usually organised into chapters or sections

2 Explore the skills

a   Read this extract from the novel *Lord of the Flies* by William Golding. As you read, jot down all of the things that you learn about the boy in the passage that are factually true. You could do this on a spider diagram to help you organise your ideas.

The boy with fair hair lowered himself down the last few feet of rock and began to pick his way toward the lagoon. Though he had taken off his school sweater and trailed it now from one hand, his grey shirt stuck to him and his hair was plastered to his forehead. All round him the long scar smashed into the jungle was a bath of heat. He was clambering heavily among the creepers and broken trunks when a bird, a vision of red and yellow, flashed upwards with a witch-like cry; and this cry was echoed by another.

William Golding, from *Lord of the Flies*

b Selecting ideas from your collected notes, answer this Paper 1, Question 1 examination task:

List four things you learn about the boy in the extract.

Checklist for success

- Present your response to Question 1 in a numbered list.
- Use short, sharp, clear sentences.
- Use only things that are stated explicitly in the extract.

③ Develop the skills

a Now go on to read the complete extract.

The boy with fair hair lowered himself down the last few feet of rock and began to pick his way toward the lagoon. Though he had taken off his school sweater and trailed it now from one hand, his grey shirt stuck to him and his hair was plastered to his forehead. All round him the long scar smashed into the jungle was a bath of heat. He was clambering heavily among the creepers and broken trunks when a bird, a vision of red and yellow, flashed upwards with a witch-like cry; and this cry was echoed by another.

'Hi!' it said. 'Wait a minute!'

The undergrowth at the side of the scar was shaken and a multitude of raindrops fell pattering.

'Wait a minute,' the voice said. 'I got caught up.'

The fair boy stopped and jerked his stockings with an automatic gesture that made the jungle seem for a moment like the Home Counties.

The voice spoke again.

'I can't hardly move with all these creeper things.'

The owner of the voice came backing out of the undergrowth so that twigs scratched on a greasy wind-breaker. The naked crooks of his knees were plump, caught and scratched by thorns. He bent down, removed the thorns carefully, and turned around. He was shorter than the fair boy and very fat. He came forward, searching out safe lodgments for his feet, and then looked up through thick spectacles.

'Where's the man with the megaphone?'

The fair boy shook his head.

'This is an island. At least I think it's an island. That's a reef out in the sea. Perhaps there aren't any grownups anywhere.'

The fat boy looked startled.

'There was that pilot. But he wasn't in the passenger cabin, he was up in front.'

The fair boy was peering at the reef through screwed-up eyes.

'All them other kids,' the fat boy went on. 'Some of them must have got out. They must have, mustn't they?'

The fair boy began to pick his way as casually as possible toward the water. He tried to be offhand and not too obviously uninterested, but the fat boy hurried after him.

'Aren't there any grownups at all?'

'I don't think so.'

(b) Look back at the quotations that have been highlighted for you in yellow. Answer the following questions.

- What clues are there here as to the kind of place the boys are in?

- Why might it be unusual for two young boys to be alone in such a place?

(c) Now look back at the quotations that have been highlighted for you in green and answer the following questions.

- What conclusions can you make about the ages of the boys and why?

- What seems to have happened to the boys for them to be stranded in this place? What is your evidence?

By now you will have made a number of **inferences** from the extract to help you get to grips with its more **implicit meanings**.

> **Key terms**
>
> **inferences:** explanations of what you have been able to read between the lines
>
> **implicit meanings:** the meanings that you have to work out by reading between the lines; things that are suggested rather than stated

(4) Final task

Using the notes you have gathered, the highlighted quotations and the inferences you have made so far, answer the following task. This builds skills for Paper 1 Question 4.

What is your impression of the situation the two boys have found themselves in?

Write up three ideas using the methods in the **Checklist for success** to show that you really understand the text. Aim to write 250–300 words in total.

Checklist for success

- Use clear statements in your own words, addressing the question directly.

- Support those statements with your selected quotations.

- Demonstrate your understanding by explaining the inferences you have made.

Working on spelling

You are learning to:
* show that you can understand some of the spelling rules of the English language and form more complex words accurately.

Testing: AO6
For: Paper 1 (and Paper 2), Question 5

1 Getting you thinking

English is made up of a whole host of words from different languages. These words have become part of our language at different times through our very varied history.

a Look at the map and think about the following questions.

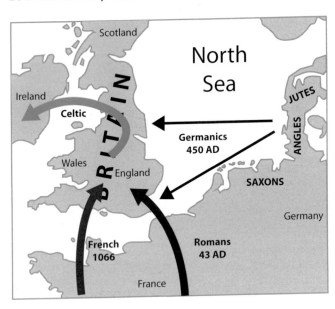

* Do you know anything about the Romans in Britain?
* Do you know who the Vikings were?
* Have you heard of the Norman Conquest?
* Can you name any places that England has ruled in the past?
* Can you think of and note down any ways these different peoples, events and places might have affected our language?

This helps to explain why English spelling can be so complicated. If English is a patchwork quilt of different languages, each one brings with it different patterns and ways of spelling.

b Using a dictionary or an online search, look up the words in bold from this opening to a piece of creative writing. Find out which language they originally came from.

Jane sat in her **pyjamas** eating leftover **cake**. She was studying for a **history** degree and could not face researching the **parliament** of James the First today.

What **adventure** could she have instead? She stirred her **coffee** and tried to summon up the energy to pull on her **jeans**. Moving her **guitar** from the bed, she looked up at her Hendrix poster – an **icon** with a **tragedy** in his story. That was history she reflected. That was all it added up to. Did she need an **expensive** degree to tell her that? She reached for the **shampoo** and headed for the shower. She could still make the 10 a.m. class.

② **Explore the skills**

Most of us have no trouble with the basic words in our language.

a Using **only** the words in the box below, write a short poem or description of a natural scene.

house	love	you	she	he	I	this	that	can	eat	sleep	live
water	leaf	moon	food	as	and	so	on	in	down	to	
when	where	day	night	shall	sun	day	winter	spring	friend		
evil	cold	then	we	us	under	up	to	heart	grass	water	
have	do	be	sky	weak	die	get	give	take			

Your poem or description is made up of familiar words, all of which are used frequently to communicate about some of the basic elements of life. They are all Anglo-Saxon or Norse in origin. Many of our everyday words come from Anglo-Saxon and are short, **monosyllabic** and logical to spell. They 'sound out' easily when you come to write them down and are made up of many of the nouns, basic verbs and pronouns used every day.

Some of our more complex words, however, tend to come from Latin: the language brought to England by the Romans around 45 BC. The Romans stayed for 300 years and brought order and organisation. Their words are very organised too.

Our Latinate vocabulary is often made up of a root word or word stem. For example:

norm

The root word changes in meaning very slightly when **prefixes** or **suffixes** are added to the beginning or end of the stem word.

e+**norm**+ous   ab+**norm**+al

Key terms

monosyllabic: a word that is made up of only one syllable, for example, 'no'

prefixes: a cluster of letters that can be added to the beginning of a word to create a new one, for example, **un** + happy

suffixes: a cluster of letters that can be added to the end of a word to create a new one, for example, sad + **ness**

b The table below gives you some common suffixes that often cause problems and confusion when spelling words. Read the golden rule in the table, then add the correct ending to the root word.

Confusing suffixes	Golden rule	Stem words	New words
–cious and –tious	If your stem ends in –ce, then lose the –ce and add –cious. If the stem ends in any other letters, remove them and add –tious.	grace space nutrition ambition	
–ation and –able	If your stem ends in –ce or –ge, keep the –e before adding –able otherwise lose the –e. Words which end in –ation can usually also use –able.	adore notice enjoy consider	

c Look at these words ending in the suffix –ible:

horrible forcible visible terrible

- Work out the stem word and write some golden rules to help you remember these suffixes.

- Think of three more –ible words to try out your rule and write each of them in a sentence.

3 Develop the skills

By thinking carefully about the word stem, you are often able to find the key to spelling other words in the same family.

For example, let's take the word **finish,** meaning the end or the limit of something.

If you can spell **finish**

↓

you can also spell **finite** by changing the ending

↓

and you can then spell **infinite** by adding a prefix

↓

you can then spell **definite** by adding a different prefix

↓

you can then create **indefinite**

↓

or **redefinition** by adding a further prefix or suffix.

a How does the meaning of the word change slightly in each of these examples? Choose three and write each one in a sentence to show its different meanings.

What does not change, however, is the spelling of the stem '**fini**'. Even if you con**fin**e yourself to learning some of these common prefixes and suffixes and their meanings, you will soon have an in**fini**te number of more complex words you can spell!

b Using the prefixes and suffixes in the table below, try to build ten more words from these Latinate stems.

equal – meaning: even or level

cure – meaning: to care

form – meaning: to shape

Examples might be:

equal: un + equal = unequal, equal + ity = equality

Common prefixes								Common suffixes	
ad	ac	as	bi	con	de	dis	in	–able	–ible
per	pre	re		trans	un			–ant	–ance
								–ent	–ence
								–acy	–ate
								–ity	–ite
								–sion	–tion

④ Final task

Read the following passage. There are six spelling errors in the complex words. Find the errors and, using your golden rules, write down the correct forms.

Exam tip

Keep a small notebook alongside your English Language notes. When you come across a new or interesting word in your studies, note it down.

- Work out how it has been built from a root word, prefixes and suffixes.

- Check its meaning online or in a dictionary.

- Use it in your own writing.

It wasn't that John was unambicious. In fact, he had enjoyed considerible success in sales. He had won the adorasion of all of his managers so far and beaten every sales target by an enormus margin. It was just lately. His performance had dropped. He woke at night with horrable nightmares that he was bottom of the target board in the office – like poor Harry had been. He looked at his sheet of appointments for the following week and wondered who he was kidding anymore...

Checklist for success

- Look closely at the way the complex words are built when you see them written down.

- Aim to remember the patterns that words create and see the links between them.

- Think twice when you are writing down complex words: have you seen a similar pattern and can you remember the root word? Use this to help you work out the correct spelling.

Working on verbs, tense and agreement

You are learning to:
- understand and think about the role of the verb in a sentence
- select the right tense of a verb so that your sentences make clear sense.

Testing: AO6
For: Paper 1 (and Paper 2), Question 5

 Getting you thinking

Verbs

A word that describes an action or a movement is called a **verb**, for example, to run, to shout, to be or to have.

A verb is also the driving force in any sentence you read, write or say. It represents, not only movements and actions, but also feelings or emotions.

A verb also shows you when things are happening, for example, in the past or the present.

Verbs are not necessarily single words. When a verb is made up of more than one word, it is called a **verb phrase**.

a Look at the extract below and think about the highlighted words and phrases. All of them are verbs. What do you notice is different about them?

- Which things happen in the past?
- Which things seem to be happening now, in the present?
- What happens when verbs are made up of more than one word?

> Snuggled in my bed, I drift back into consciousness. Then, the numbers on the clock leap out at me. I have slept in, yet again. Stumbling down the stairs, I grab a quick coffee before heading for the bus. Then I realise. Outside the rain is torrential. It is going to be one of those days, yet again.

 Explore the skills

Tenses

The verbs in a text don't *just* communicate actions. They help you to make sense of the time in which things are happening. This is called the **tense** of the verb.

Verbs can tell you about things which are happening in the present.

Texts that contain the present tense often have an immediate 'here and now' feel about them – as though you were almost witnessing what is happening as you read.

a Read this extract from *The Generation Game* by Sophie Duffy where she describes a memory of school.

> School is more bearable now I have Lucas for a friend. He might only be small and thin but he has a voice that even Miss Pitchfork must envy. A voice like a crow having a bad day. A voice he uses sparingly, for greater effect.
>
> Lucas and I soon settle into a shared routine that gets us through the six hour long haul. We play together at break in our corner. We pick each other for teams in gym. I save a place for him on the carpet. He saves a place for me in the hall at lunchtime where I give him my greens in exchange for potatoes.
> (He is a boy of mystery.)
>
> Sophie Duffy, from *The Generation Game*

b Make a list of all of the present tense verbs in the passage. Are they single word verbs or verb phrases?

c Thinking about the topic of the passage, why do you think the writer chose to use the present tense? Why did she use such simple verbs to convey the actions of the school day?

Auxiliary verbs

Other verbs, such as '**to have**' and '**to be**', are not so simple.

These verbs have other jobs to do in a sentence, as well as being verbs in their own right. They assist other verbs to communicate actions and time much more specifically.

When they assist other verbs they are called **auxiliaries**. You need to use the correct forms of these verbs for your writing to make sense.

If you look at the present tense of the verb 'to have' in the table, it looks straightforward, but when you change its tense you notice different patterns.

d Using the examples to help you, complete the tables.

Present tense: 'to have'	Simple past tense	Future tense
I have		
You have		You will have
S/he has	S/he had	
We have		
They have		

Present tense: 'to be'	Simple past tense	Future tense
I am You are S/he is We are They are	You were	I will be

Both 'to have' and 'to be' help you to form special past tenses. The verb 'to have' is used when you want to indicate something that has ended but is only recently finished:

Phew! I have found my keys.

It is also used to indicate that something in the past has been going on for a long period of time.

She has taken flowers to the grave every week since he died.

e Write five sentences using the verb 'to have' as an auxiliary.

- I have…
- You have…
- S/he has…
- We have…
- They have…

The verb 'to be' indicates that something was continuing to happen in the past. This can be very useful when writing your own stories, for example:

I **was travelling** on the stretch of lonely road when…

We **were marching** onwards into the night, with no idea of where we were heading.

f Write five sentences using the verb 'to be' as an auxiliary.

- I was…
- You were…
- S/he was…
- We were…
- They were…

The key thing to remember is always to match the pronoun with the correct form of the verb. This is called **agreement**.

'We was marching…' will always be incorrect! 'Was' is for **one** person or thing. 'Were' is for **more than one**.

3 Develop the skills

It can be tricky to choose the correct form of a verb in writing because we often speak more informally, or use a particular regional accent.

a Rewrite the following transcript into formal Standard English.

b Make some notes on the changes you have made. Explain why confusion might occur between the spoken forms and the Standard English written forms.

Jack: We was much better off in the old days.
Bill: No doubt about it. I were much happier without computers and mobile phones and all that technology.
Jack: My grandson, he were here the other day and he was never off his phone.
Bill: I were on the bus the other day and there was a young lad just the same. Tap, tapping away.
Jack: In our day, we just talked to each other. We was proper sociable.
Bill: Mind you, Jack, you was always a chatterbox…never shutting up. I might have preferred hearing from you by text message!

4 Final task

Rewrite this extract, also from *The Generation Game*, but this time change the present tense to the past tense.

Sometimes Lucas and I are given complete and utter freedom, freedom that would never be contemplated these days for six-year-olds without serious concerns for their health and safety. We like to wander the local streets. We like to go down the road to Toy Town with our pocket money to add to our growing collection of Dinky TV tie-ins. We like to call in to see Mr Bob Sugar who stocks us up with goodies…. we like to spend hours playing Hide-and-Seek amongst the crosses and angels or Guess-the-Animal-Poo amongst the shrubs and undergrowth. But the time I am happiest in the Bone Yard is when Lucas helps me with my reading. I have mastered several Biblical verses and all the old family names of Torquay. He is a good teacher.

Checklist for success

- Practise the use of the three past tenses in your task: the simple past, the past perfect and the past imperfect.

- Ensure you use the correct auxiliary, where needed.

Introducing narrative structure

You are learning to:
- understand what narrative writing is and how it can be structured
- explore how professional writers use narrative structure effectively.

Testing: AO5
For: Paper 1 Question 5

1 Getting you thinking

Being creative and writing when you are under pressure in an exam can seem daunting. The important thing to remember is that stories surround you most of the time and that you can weave a story effectively with very little prompting.

a Think about the last time you sat down with a friend to chat. What did you talk about?

Chances are, you talked about something that had happened to one or both of you or someone you know. In that case, you were telling a story.

b Think about an advertisement you have seen on television recently, or a music video that 'tells a story'. Jot down the elements you can remember.

- Do you meet any characters?
- Are they in a specific location?
- What message are you being given – is there a simple plot?

2 Explore the skills

A written story is called **narrative writing**. In the examination, you will be given the choice of writing one of two tasks based on different **purposes**. One of the purposes is to **narrate**.

When you are writing a narrative, you need to attract the attention of your reader or **audience** immediately. In short story writing, you have only a limited amount of time to deliver the whole plot.

Sometimes you will be asked to write just the opening of a story or part of a story in the exam. Sometimes you will be asked to write a complete story.

Key terms

narrative writing: a written story

purposes: the 'job' your piece of writing is doing, for example, narrating, describing, persuading

narrate: tell a story

audience: the person or people you are writing for; your readership

a   Look at the extract below where a student is writing
about an unhappy relationship.

> Susan was really miserable with Andy. They had
> been married for ten years but had no children.
> They lived quite comfortably in a flat on the edge of
> a trendy town and Susan had a job as a secretary.
> Andy worked in sales and was away from home a
> lot. Susan sat in the flat every night and thought
> about the past. She looked through their wedding
> photos and thought about how happy they were
> then and how...

b   Now look at this opening from a short story,
'Gazebo,' by Raymond Carver on the same topic.

> That morning she pours Teacher's over my belly and
> licks it off. That afternoon she tries to jump out of
> the window.
>
>   Raymond Carver, 'Gazebo' from *What we talk about when we*
>   *talk about love*

- How does the Carver opening suggest this is about a relationship?
- What do you notice about who is telling the story in each case?
- Which one invites you to ask more questions or sets up a mystery? How is that achieved?
  Make a note of the questions it raises for you.
- Which one has engaged your interest more quickly and why?
- Rewrite the first story opening in only three sentences to make it more engaging and
  interesting.

c   Now look at this opening from the short story 'Roof Space' by David Grubb.

> I am up here in the roof space. I am Michael.
>
>   David Grubb, 'Roof Space' from *Best British Short Stories 2014*

- What has the writer managed to establish for you in two sentences?
- What questions is he inviting you to ask?

d Now read the next paragraph.

> I am waiting for my father to come up into this space above where we live. To join me with the tracks and trains, the arrivals and departures, the timetabled lives, these journeys.

- What do you learn very quickly?
- What age do you imagine for the person narrating the story?
- What other questions does this now set up for you?

Grubb goes on to write:

> I am up here in the roof space and when my father arrives there will be announcements and whistles and precision and everything will work and for hours at a time we will be in command.
>
> Not like downstairs. Not like the house beneath. Not like the rooms and the demands and the crying. Not like the father then.

Very quickly we are given an impression of a relationship and a household.

- What do you learn about the boy and the father?
- What do you learn about the household?
- Spend a few minutes thinking about this opening and jot down some notes on where you think this story will go. What story does Michael want to tell you?

This paragraph sets up a way for the story to gain momentum, to build up the action. This is part of the classic formula or five-point structure of story writing.

 3 Develop the skills

Structuring a story

Look at the diagram. It presents the classic formula of story writing.

After the opening, you expect some kind of build-up in the momentum of a story, reaching an important or pivotal moment – the climax. This could be the key moment of tension for the reader, a dramatic incident or a moment when you come to realise something very important.

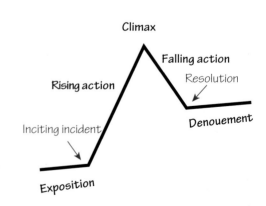

a Read this extract from 'The Mirrored Twins' by Jackie Kay.

> The fog was really dense now, you could cut it with an ice axe. Both men climbed down into it. Slabs and slabs of fog. It was cold on their faces, wet, damp. Hamish was behind Don; momentarily, he had let him out of his sight. He started to panic; he couldn't see Don. 'Let's just get down,' he shouted. He was feeling a little breathless, and light-headed. A little odd. He wasn't quite sure what was the matter with him. He didn't want to mention anything to Don because he was a bit of a worrier, Don. [...] But Don being Don, sensed something, maybe something in his voice, and shouted, 'Are you all right? Do you think we should rope up? I'll come back up and you go first then I can keep an eye on you.'
>
> Don turned round and started climbing back towards Hamish and lost his footing. The rocks under him scrambled and gave way to him and he felt himself slide and slip and tumble...
>
> Jackie Kay, 'The Mirrored Twins' from *Wish I Was Here*

b Make a bullet-pointed plan of what might have happened leading up to this climactic moment. Answer these questions a reader might have: Who are Don and Hamish and how do they know each other? What is different about their characters and skills? Where are they? Why are they on this trip?

c Write the possible next paragraph of this story. What do you imagine happened next? (the falling action)

④ Final task

a Write an effective opening paragraph for a short story using the title 'The Visit' as your prompt.

b Complete a plan for the rest of your story using the classic structure formula shown in the example on the right.

Checklist for success

- Begin in a concise way without too much 'background'.
- Establish a character or narrator and location quickly.
- Allow your reader to ask questions in the opening which you will answer as your plot unfolds.

> Introduction:
> Character is on a train returning to home town after a long time away...
>
> Complication:
>
> Rising action:
>
> Climax:
>
> Resolution:

Planning and writing a structured narrative

You are learning to:
- plan an examination-style story writing task using an effective structure
- write up your complete story supported by a professional writer's model example.

Testing: AO5
For: Paper 1 Question 5

① Getting you thinking

For Question 5, you may be asked to write a narrative: perhaps a short story, or an extract from a novel.

In the examination, you need to be organised and decide where you are heading. You do not have lots of time to think and change aspects of your story.

a Look at the possible examination task below.

> **Write a story about a memorable day you spent with friends.**
>
> Jot down two or three memories from your own experience. Could any of them be adapted into a short story?
>
> Consider:
> - would you alter your friends' names?
> - would you keep the same location?
> - what was interesting/dramatic/tense about the events of that day?

b Choose one of your ideas.
Spend five minutes constructing the basic five-point plan.
For example:

> **My memory:** The time we went on a girls' day out to the races.
>
> **Introduction:** Set the scene as to how cold it was/no one really enjoying themselves.
>
> **Complication:** Discovering everything was really expensive
>
> **Rising action:**
>
> **Climax:**
>
> **Resolution:**

② **Explore the skills**

a Read this opening from the short story 'Ladies' Day' by Vicki Jarrett. Make notes on the questions in the annotations.

A wet, gusty wind barges across the race track and slaps the crowd for being daft enough to have pictured this day as sunny.

The women, the *ladies*, are woefully exposed to the elements in thin dresses that flick and snap around goose-bumped fake tan, not a coat to be seen, clinging on to head gear, reinserting clips and pins, trying to hold it all together against the odds.

Three of us from the baby group – me, Kaz and Ashley – shelter behind a bookies' booth.

'Remind me again why we're here,' says Ashley, leaning on my shoulder for balance as she picks a wad of muddy grass from the heel of her stiletto.

Kaz glares at her. 'We're here to have a day off. Away from the kids, the husbands, the housework and everything. We're going to have fun, right?' She scowls at the two of us until we nod agreement.

Vicki Jarrett, 'Ladies' Day' from *Best British Short Stories 2014*

Think about how quickly the writer has set the scene, location and atmosphere. What will they be like in your story?

What details are used here to create an impression of the weather? Can you visualise this scene? Is it realistic? What details would add to the picture you want to create in your opening?

What do you notice about the names of the characters and the snippet of dialogue? What do they add? How do you know the women are disappointed already with their day out? What were they expecting?

How does this short bit of dialogue answer questions for the reader? What do you now know about the characters? Will you include dialogue in your opening?

---

b Write the first 100–150 words of your story.

Aim:

- for a crisp, concise opening
- to establish your characters, setting and atmosphere.

Now you need to add a **complication** to your story whilst still remaining clear and concise.

In Vicki Jarrett's story, the day at the races is expensive and the women don't have a lot of money.

c   Here is how she establishes this **complication**:

> Two plastic cups of fizzy wine pretending to be champagne and a double vodka later, the weather isn't so bad.
>
> 'Another?' I wave my empty cup at the others. I'd be feeling quite relaxed if it wasn't for these heels.
>
> 'Nah. These prices are ridiculous,' says Kaz. 'Ashley, phone your Barry and get him to pass something over the fence for us.'

- How do we get a sense that the day isn't as glamorous as it's supposed to be?
- What does the writer do to really give us a sense of realistic characters?
- What's implied by 'pass something over the fence for us'?

d   Write another paragraph of your story to introduce a possible complication. Think carefully about:

- details
- using the voice of your characters or narrator to add realism.

Aim to write 50–75 words.

③ Develop the skills

As Vicki Jarrett's story reaches its climax, we come to realise something important about the characters.

a   Make some notes on:

- how the writer manages time and tense in this extract
- how the writer connects the experiences of the women with the horse racing.

> An hour later, Ashley sits cross-legged on the tartan rug, one strap hanging off her shoulder, talking about her Barry and how he's great with the twins but the house will be a bombsite when she gets back because he can't multi-task. When she starts talking in circles, Kaz takes over about her dad's cancer and how her brother's no help at all since their mum's gone [...] She talks fast, eyes wide, lips wet with vodka and Coke. I think she'd like to stop talking because now she's rounded the last turn and we can all see what's waiting on the finish line. [...] None of us are used to talking without constant interruption from children. Combined with the drink, it's like running too fast downhill.
>
> The horses thunder past...

b Think carefully about the climax to your story. How will you present it? Is it a moment of importance or realisation – such as the one in this story; or a moment of tension and drama such as the one in 'The Mirrored Twins' (see Week 4, Lesson 1).

Write up your climactic moment using approximately 150 words.

④ Final task

A short story is often like a snapshot moment of a life experience or event. Writers can pack concentrated ideas into a short piece of fiction and often leave us with a key message or something to think about in their endings.

a Read this ending to 'Ladies' Day' and the notes in the annotations. Notice how the tone shifts from being very chatty to quite serious and formal as the narrator watches a horse head to the finish line.

> She's out in front and my heart starts beating faster as I watch her straining ahead, a hurtling mass of muscle and sweat. She's tearing through the air, ripping it apart. It's like she's trying to tear a hole in front of her and escape through it, to some other place where something else, something more is waiting, a place where maybe she can stop running. It's always that bit further ahead. The promise of that.

The writer shifts the attention back to the horse race.

Is this what the women were trying to do on their day out?

How does this match with what you have learned about the lives of the characters?

What message does the writer give us about life and its pressures?

b Think about the ending of your story – is there a key thought or message you would like to give your reader about your memorable day?

For example:

- a message about friendship
- a warning about dangers or risks
- an encouragement to live life to the fullest.

c Complete your story, adding in any further sentences necessary to link your drafted work together.

Checklist for success

- Ensure your story has an effective opening, a complication, a climax and resolution.
- Ensure you have paragraphed each of these shifts clearly.

Developing skills with sentences and punctuation

1 Getting you thinking

Sentence punctuation

a Look at these sentences and decide what is different about each one.

> Have we got any homework tonight?
>
> Tuesday is homework night.
>
> Homework is a total nightmare!
>
> Get that homework done now.

Each sentence here has a different job to do. The different functions are as follows:

- making a **statement**
- asking a question or making a request
- giving a **command**
- making an **exclamation**.

b Match the sentences above to their correct function. These are **sentence forms**.

c Read the extract below from the novel *Junk* by Melvin Burgess. In it, the character Gemma has been in a disagreement with her parents.

Key terms

statement: a sentence that declares something and presents it as a fact or opinion

command: a sentence that tells us to do something by putting the verb first to emphasise the action

exclamation: a sentence that expresses an emotion such as shock, anger or surprise

---

I didn't go back that day. In fact, I stayed away all weekend as a protest.

Response: banned from going out of the house at weekends.

My next plot was to stay out until ten each night during the week. They couldn't keep me off school in the name of discipline, surely? They got round that by my dad picking me up from school. My God! Everyone knew what was going on. He actually came into the class to get me! I thought I was going to die of humiliation.

Melvin Burgess, from *Junk*

- What form does each sentence in the extract have?
- What do the statements provide for us?

- Who is the question addressed to?
- What tone do the exclamations suggest? What mood is Gemma in?
- What is the benefit for the writer in being able to use different sentence forms?

② Explore the skills

Long ago, early forms of writing had no punctuation at all. Not everyone could write and those who could did not even use spaces between their words.

(a) Try reading this extract from *Junk*. Is it as straightforward to read and understand as the extract in Activity 1?

ThisishowIdiditIhidmybaginagardenafewdoorsdownonFridaynightsoIwouldntgetseenwalking outwithitnextmorningshowerbreakfastwhereareyougoingthis weekendmydaddemandedhe ddroppedthepretenceoflikingmeoverthepastfewweeksIshruggeddowntownmaybehesnortedmy mumleanedacrossandheldmyarmstayoutoftroubleGemmashebeggedbutIdidntevenbother lookingatherIthoughtifonlyyouknewIsneakedoutabouttenMumwasupstairsanddadwasout atthesupermarketIwalkedoutofthehouseanddowntheroadtothecoachstation

(b) Make a copy of the passage on a large sheet of paper, inserting the spaces between the words.

Think about the four sentence forms you learned about earlier.

Which sentence form ends with:

- **?** a question mark
- **!** an exclamation mark?

The remaining two sentence forms end with full stops.

Add the correct sentence punctuation in to your copy using a coloured pen.

Already, you should start to see the passage beginning to make more sense, but other types of punctuation also help make writing clearer.

Apostrophes of omission

Apostrophes help us to create clear meaning in two ways.

Apostrophes of omission pinpoint where we have joined two words together to make a more informal version. If someone sends you an email asking for the arrangements for a party, you are unlikely to reply with:

I do not know. It has not been decided yet.

Much more likely would be:

I don't know. We haven't sorted it out yet.

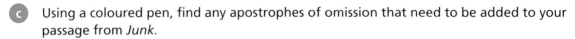

Apostrophes help you to create that friendly, informal tone. The apostrophe replaces the letters you have missed out or omitted.

The general rule is:

- identify which letters are removed
- join the words back together with the apostrophe.

c Using a coloured pen, find any apostrophes of omission that need to be added to your passage from *Junk*.

Apostrophes of possession

The second way apostrophes add clarity to your writing is by showing belonging.

These are known as **apostrophes of possession**.

These apostrophes change their place depending on whether you are showing belonging to one person or thing, or many.

For example:

> The boy's books

places the apostrophe straight after the word 'boy' and before the 's'. This tells you there is only one boy and all the books belong to him.

However:

> The boys' books

places the apostrophe after the 's' of 'boys'.

This tells us there is a group of boys with books belonging to all of them.

 ③ Develop the skills

Commas

Commas form a mini break or boundary in a sentence where you want to separate different aspects of an idea or description.

This table gives some of the most common uses of the comma.

Use of comma	Example
Commas are used to separate out the items in a list.	I couldn't decide between the chocolate eclairs, the strawberry tarts, the vanilla slices – they all looked delicious.
Commas are used to link adjectives when more than one is used to describe something.	The thrashing, pounding waves made a dramatic sight on the beach.
At the beginning of a sentence they create a pause after names, discourse markers or answers like 'yes' and 'no'.	Alex, can you stop playing on the computer now. However, the story ends happily. Yes, it's going to be a good day.
They can be used in pairs to drop extra pieces of information into a sentence.	The river, which was polluted, burst its banks and flooded the nearby village.

a   Look at the examples provided and then write an example of your own for each usage.

Speech punctuation

When characters are in conversation with each other in a novel or short story, this is called **dialogue**.

We present the words they speak in speech marks. However, other punctuation marks are also used alongside the speech marks. Look at these punctuation marks and answer the questions.

What do you notice about what the dialogue begins with?

What happens when a new speaker begins to speak?

'Are you absolutely serious?' Phil said.

'Of course,' Sheila replied, 'I'm deadly serious.'

Where does the sentence punctuation go?

What is needed when the speaker hasn't finished speaking?

b   Look back at the extract from *Junk*. Add in any commas to clarify the meaning. Add any speech punctuation to show where Gemma is using dialogue.

What is needed before the speaker begins again?

④ Final task

a   There are 22 punctuation marks missing in this passage from the novel *The Girl With the Dragon Tattoo* by Stieg Larsson.
The sentence punctuation is in place, but the following have been left out:

- apostrophes
- commas
- speech marks.

Identify where all the missing punctuation marks go, using the rules you have just learned.

Salander was dressed for the day in a black T-shirt with a picture on it of E.T. with fangs and the words I am also an alien. She had on a black skirt that was frayed at the hem a worn-out black mid-length leather jacket rivet belt heavy Doc Marten boots and horizontally striped green-and-red knee socks. She had put on make-up in a colour scheme that indicated she might be colour-blind. In other words she was exceptionally decked out. [...]
This is Ms Salendar who prepared the report. Armansky hesitated a second and then went on with a smile that was intended to engender confidence but which seemed helplessly apologetic. Dont be fooled by her youth. She is our absolute best researcher.
Im persuaded of that Frode said in a dry tone that hinted at the opposite. Tell me what she found out.

Stieg Larsson, from *The Girl With the Dragon Tattoo*

Developing skills with sentence structure and variety

You are learning to:
- understand the different ways sentences are built or structured
- consider the effect of different sentence structures.

Testing: AO6
For: Paper 1 (and Paper 2) Question 5

① Getting you thinking

You've discovered already that sentences can take different **forms**. They can also have different **structures**. Varying these can add to the impact of a piece of writing and create special effects within it.

 a Look at the sentences below. They are all on the same topic.

> **A** I like reading.
>
> **B** I hate reading, so I listen to texts on my mp3 player.
>
> **C** I liked reading until I had to read that awful book in school.
>
> **D** I hate reading usually, but that book, which we read in class, was totally brilliant.

- Look at sentences A and C. What is the main idea in each?
- Look at sentence B. If you took out the word 'so' and changed the comma to a full stop would the ideas still make sense?
- Look at sentence C. If you took out the word 'until' and added a full stop, would the two ideas make sense together?
- What are the two key ideas in sentence D? Which part of the sentence provides additional information to us?

The four sentences above are the four main ways we can build or structure sentences in English. Their names are:

simple	complex
compound-complex	compound

Look back at the sentences above and try to decide which label belongs with which sentence. Decide how each one got its name.

Explore the skills

Simple sentences

A **simple sentence**:

- contains one idea

- has one verb or verb phrase

- has one action, event or state within it

- contains at least one noun or **pronoun** that is linked or attached to the verb.

<blockquote>**Key term**

pronoun: a word such as I, he, she, we, they or it that replaces a noun in a sentence</blockquote>

For example:

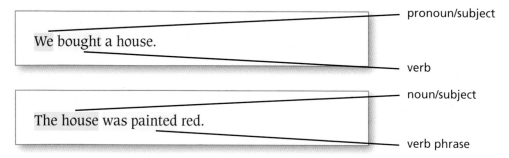

We bought a house. — pronoun/subject ... verb

The house was painted red. — noun/subject ... verb phrase

Simple sentences tend to be quite short, punchy and terse. They can create a clipped effect in a text. They can often indicate a kind of tension. Simple sentences are not necessarily 'easy to read' or understand. The simplicity is linked to their structure, not their ideas.

a Read this extract from the short story, 'Everything Stuck to Him' by Raymond Carver, then complete the tasks below.

> They stared at each other.[1] Then the boy took up his hunting gear and went outside.[2] He started the car.[3] He went around to the car windows and, making a job of it, scraped away the ice.[4]
>
> He turned off the motor and sat awhile.[5] And then he got out and went back inside.[6]
>
> The living-room light was on.[7] The girl was asleep on the bed.[8] The baby was asleep beside her.[9]
>
> The boy took off his boots.[10]
>
> Raymond Carver, 'Everything Stuck to Him'

- Identify all of the verbs and verb phrases in the extract.

- Identify the six **simple sentences** in the extract.

- Look carefully at sentence 1 and then sentence 10. What tension do you detect in the story? What has changed from the beginning of the extract to the end?

- Now look closely at the remaining sentences and make notes on why they are not **simple**.

- Look at sentences 2, 5 and 6. How does the writer link the two ideas in each sentence?

Compound sentences

Sentences 2, 5 and 6 are **compound sentences**. A compound sentence happens when two simple sentences with linked ideas are joined together. They are joined with co-ordinating **conjunctions**.

Key term

conjunctions: joining words or connectives such as for, and, nor, but, or, yet, so

For example:

pronoun

verb

We bought a house **and** painted it red.

A conjunction joins the ideas. No second noun or pronoun is needed as we know what is being referred to.

A second verb is needed, though, to show the second action and idea.

A common mistake is to join two simple sentences together without using a conjunction:

We bought a house, it was painted red.

This is called a 'comma splice' and is not considered an accurate way to build or punctuate a sentence.

3 Develop the skills

Complex sentences

A **complex sentence** still has, at its core, a simple sentence. However, it develops the idea contained in the simple sentence and adds more detail and information in little subsections.

For example:

It was way back in '56 that **we bought the house,** painted it up in a pillar box red and planted out the garden.

The subsections *depend* on the simple sentence, as they don't make sense on their own.

The simple sentence is still at the core of the sentence and makes sense in its own right.

The subsections add to the idea and provide more detail, and more information about time, place or manner.

In a complex sentence, the simple sentence becomes known as the **main clause**.

The subsections become known as the **subordinate clauses** as they can't make sense alone, without the main clause.

Complex sentences can take us on a journey of thoughts, to create a vivid picture in our minds. They are not necessarily difficult to understand! The complexity comes from the type of journey we are taken on.

a Rewrite the passage from 'Everything Stuck to Him', changing the six simple sentences into complex sentences by adding subordinate clauses, telling us something about time, place or manner.

For example:

> For a good while, **they stared at each other**, anger and resentment behind their eyes.

b When you have finished your rewrite, explore the differences the changes in sentence structure make to the text. What is added? What is taken away? How has the tension changed?

④ Final task

You've discovered already that sentences can be structured in different ways.

These structures can add to the impact of a text and create special effects within it. One of these sentences is a **minor sentence**, and the other is a complex sentence.

> So listen.

Key term

minor sentence: a sentence that lacks one or more of the elements that go to make up a full sentence, for example, a subject or a main verb

> He traverses streets of dirty, straggling houses, with now and then an unexpected court composed of buildings as ill-proportioned and deformed as the half-naked children that wallow in the kennels.

a Which sentence gives you more detail and description?

b Which one forces you to stop?

c Which one has the slowest pace? How does it do this?

d Which one creates the most drama and tension?

e Which one creates the most visual image in your mind's eye?

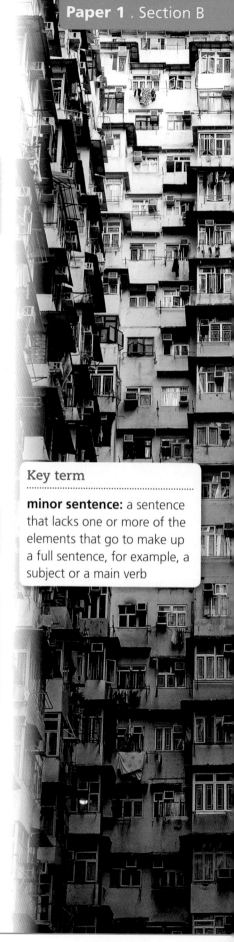

Planning and writing a narrative opening from a picture stimulus

You are learning to:
- understand how professional writers create effective openings to novels
- plan and write an examination-style novel opening task
- plan and write an examination-style task inspired by a picture.

Testing: AO5
For: Paper 1 Question 5

① Getting you thinking

One of the choices you may have in the examination is to write a story based on an image: a picture or a photograph.

A good way to start is to look at the picture like a detective and ask yourself as many questions as you can about what you see.

a Look at the painting on the right and jot down the questions it raises for you as you look at it.

Perhaps your first questions were about the woman in the picture or the place itself.

② Explore the skills

a Now look at the possible examination task below.

Write the opening extract of a novel based on the picture above.

Just as in a short story, the *opening* to a novel should set up:
- character
- situation
- location.

It should also raise important questions to keep readers hooked.

(b) Look at the questions below, gathered by a group of students. Answer them yourself to form your own interpretation of what's happening in the picture. Record your ideas in a spider diagram or a structured list. This will form an outline plan for the examination task above.

- Who is the woman? What is she wearing? Does she work there or is she just in the fashion of the time? Why is she waiting there?

- What is the building and where is it? Is that a film that's showing? What is the film? How long has it been on? Why is the woman not watching the film? Who else is there?

- What is the light like in this place and the fabrics and furnishings? Is this modern or in the past? When is this?

Once you have gathered your initial thoughts and ideas, you have some choices to make as a writer. One of the most important choices is whether you will choose a **first-person** or a **third-person narrator**. This will decide whether your story is told from the point of view of a character in the story or not.

(c) Read this student's opening to the examination task set earlier using a **third-person narrator**.

Sandy leaned against the wall and checked her watch. Seven forty-five. The film had started fifteen minutes earlier even though the place was half empty on this rainy November night. A handful of people occupied the plush red velvet seats. A couple on a first date. Two elderly women – regulars every Wednesday – and a few lonely figures. As lonely perhaps as Sandy, leaning against the wall and waiting by the stairs.

(d) Now rewrite the paragraph above as though *you* were Sandy. Think about what you can include now that the third-person narrative is left out. You could begin:

I stepped back, out of the shadows and into the faded golden light…

Key terms
....

first-person narrator: when a character in a story tells it in their voice using 'I'. This makes it feel like they are sharing their experiences with you

third-person narrator: when a story is told objectively using 'he', 'she', 'they'. This can make it feel like an outside observer is telling the story, looking in

e   When you have finished, decide which narrative perspective or point of view might be more effective in presenting the character in the picture.

③ Explore the skills

In a novel opening, you may not always have a specific event happening, but you could have a glimpse of an interesting person or place.

a   Read this opening to a novel by Linda Grant called *The Clothes on Their Backs* published in 2008. Investigate the interesting glimpses the writer gives you by answering the questions in the annotations. There are no right or wrong answers.

This morning, for the first time in many years, I passed the shop on Seymour Street. I saw the melancholy sign in the window which announced that it was closing down and through the glass the rails on which the clothes hung, half abandoned, as if the dresses and coats, blouses and sweaters had fled in the night, vanished down the street, flapping their empty arms.

> What does this suggest about where the character has been?

> Why might this particular shop be important?

> What feeling is being established?

There was Eunice, behind the counter, patting her blue-black lacquered hair with silver nails. How old she looked, and how forlorn, her chin sinking for a moment on her chest. [...]

> What is assumed by just using a character's first name?

> What image does she have and how does this contrast with how she is feeling? Why might she feel like this?

An impulse took me through the door, a strong pang of sympathy. I stepped inside and her perfume filled the room, inimitably Eunice – Revlon's Aquamarine, the scent of eau de nil and gold.

> How well must the narrator know the character of Eunice? What might their relationship be?

Linda Grant, from *The Clothes on Their Backs*

b   Think about how you could create an interesting focus in your story through adding small details about the character. Make some notes on:

- what the character looks like
- how she is positioned against the wall
- the details on her clothing and shoes
- the shadows and the way the light falls on her.

c Write a paragraph in **third-person narrative** describing what you see. Or you could write from the point of view of someone observing her – as in the Linda Grant extract – perhaps someone watching the film whose attention is caught by the character. You could begin:

> She was leaning against the wall in the golden lamplight, a faint shadow surrounding her ...

d Go on to look more closely by zooming in on the details in the picture you are given.

Use these observations to help you include interesting features in your creative writing. For example:

> Her bluntly cut blonde hair was caught in the yellow light until she almost disappeared into the yellow wallpaper behind.

Write two more sentences of your own focusing in on:

- her facial expression
- the position of her hand.

4 Final task

a Using the plan and the ideas you have gathered, write a response to the examination task.

Write the opening extract of a novel based on the picture above.

Checklist for success

- Choose a narrative perspective (first or third person) and ensure you stick to it right the way through.
- Aim to include some interesting or unusual glimpses into character and location.
- Zoom in on some smaller details to engage your readers.

Half-term progress assessment task: narrative writing

You are aiming to show that:
- you can select and plan an examination task testing narrative writing
- you can organise and structure your piece of narrative writing effectively
- you can include some accurate, complex spellings
- you can control the tense of your verbs and agreement
- you can punctuate your work in a way that shows you are clear and accurate
- you can vary your sentences for effect.

Testing: AO5 and AO6
For: Paper 1 Question 5 Creative writing

What you can expect in the exam

In Paper 1 Section B of your exam, you will be asked to complete a piece of creative writing. The topic will be based on the extract of fiction you have read and answered questions on in Section A. It is a 45-minute task, but is worth 40 marks in total – half of the marks for the paper.

You are able to earn 24 marks for the **content and organisation** of your work.

You are able to earn 16 marks for the **technical accuracy** of your work.

You could be given:

- a choice between two **narrative tasks** such as the ones you have been working on in Weeks 5 and 6

- a choice of a **narrative task and a descriptive task**

- a choice between **two descriptive tasks**.

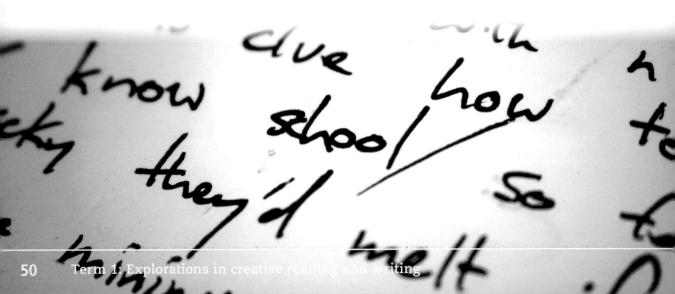

Step 1

This is the type of mark scheme that will be used to mark the **content and organisation** of your work for Question 5. Use the annotations to help you to understand exactly what the examiner is looking for.

Key terms

Register: the choice of vocabulary, grammar and style you make for your audience, for example, formal or informal

discourse markers: words or phrases that help to organise your writing into sections. For example: nevertheless, however, so

AO5 Content and organisation	
Upper Level 3 16–18 marks **'Consistent'**	**Content** • **Register** is consistently matched to audience • Consistently matched to purpose • Increasingly sophisticated vocabulary chosen for effect; range of successful linguistic devices **Organisation** • Effective structural features • Engaging with a range of clear, connected ideas • Coherent paragraphs; integrated **discourse markers**
Lower Level 3 13–15 marks **'Clear'**	**Content** • Register is generally matched to **audience** • Generally matched to **purpose** • **Vocabulary** clearly chosen for effect; appropriate linguistic devices **Organisation** • Usually effective **structural features** • Engaging with a range of **connected ideas** • Usually coherent **paragraphs**; a range of discourse markers
Upper Level 2 10–12 marks **'Some success'**	**Content** • Sustained attempt to match register to audience • Sustained attempt to match purpose • Conscious use of vocabulary; some linguistic devices **Organisation** • Some structural features • Variety of linked, relevant ideas • Some paragraphs and discourse markers
Lower Level 2 7–12 marks **'Attempts'**	**Content** • Attempts to match register to audience • Attempts to match purpose • Begins to vary vocabulary; some linguistic devices **Organisation** • Attempts structural features • Some linked, relevant ideas • Attempts paragraphs with some discursive markers

Are you writing in a way which would be acceptable to your reader, using the right tone to engage them without being offensive or inappropriate?

Have you remembered if you are narrating a story or doing a description and stuck to it right the way through? (You will learn more about describing next half term.)

Are you choosing words to interest your reader? Can you use language special effects such as similes and metaphors? (You will learn more about this next half term.)

Are you using some of the features a real writer uses to add interest to the structure such as shifts in time or flashbacks, patterns such as repetition, effective and coherent openings and endings?

Are you organising your work into paragraphs to show where the topic changes in your writing?

Look at the section of the mark scheme highlighted in yellow.

If you follow the ladder of skills in the bullet points it suggests you need to:

- ✓ remember to use **paragraphs** to organise your work or other interesting ways to **structure** your piece of writing

- ✓ include a good selection of interesting **vocabulary**

- ✓ make good **choices of language**, special effects. Use **interesting details** to create characters and impressions of places just like the professional writers' work you have been reading so far on the course.

Step 2

Choose **one** of the examination tasks below.

Either:

Write a **short story** using the title 'The Lost Boy'.

Or:

Write the **opening chapter of a novel** inspired by the photograph below.

Or:

Write a **short story** about a group of friends who become lost whilst exploring an unknown place.

You have 45 minutes to complete this task.

Spend 5–10 minutes planning your task using the method you learned in Week 5.

Introduction:

Complication:

Rising action:

Climax:

Resolution:

Step 3

Write up your narrative in no more than 25–30 minutes.

Step 4

You are now going to check the accuracy of your writing using the mark scheme grid that an examiner will use to check your work.

In an examination situation you would have 5–10 minutes of time left to check your work. However, bear in mind that there are 16 marks at stake here. Look carefully at what is required for **Level 3** and above in order for work to be **'clear'**.

Work carefully through your narrative, using the questions below to help you achieve maximum accuracy. In this practice, there is no set time limit for the task.

Note here that the ladder of skills includes:

* two bullet points that focus on your **choices of words** and how you **spell** them

* two bullet points that focus on your **control of grammar** and ability to vary your **sentences**

* two bullet points that focus on how you **punctuate** your work.

Level	Skills descriptors
Level 3 9–12 marks **'Clear'**	• Sentence demarcation is mostly secure and mostly accurate —————— • Range of punctuation is used, mostly with success —————— • Uses a variety of sentence forms for effect —————— • Mostly uses Standard English appropriately with mostly controlled grammatical structures —————— • Generally accurate spelling, including complex and irregular words —————— • Increasingly sophisticated use of vocabulary ——————
Level 2 5–8 marks **'Some'** **'Attempts'**	• Sentence demarcation is mostly secure and sometimes accurate • Some control of a range of punctuation • Attempts a variety of sentence forms • Some use of Standard English with some control of agreement • Some accurate spelling of more complex words • Varied use of vocabulary

Have I ensured all of my sentences are marked with a full stop, or, if required, an exclamation mark or a question mark?

Have I used commas in lists, perhaps tried a colon or semi-colon, remembered to put any dialogue into speech marks? Have I used apostrophes correctly?

Have I used different types of sentences to add variety to my work to create a different pace, add surprise, drama, tension, detail?

Have I written in Standard English and thought carefully about using the right tenses and auxiliary verbs?

Are all of my basic spellings okay and the tricky words I have used as good as I can get them?

Am I trying to use more imaginative and complex words?

Check your progress

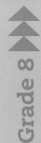

Grade 8

- I can communicate with impact.
- I can produce an ambitious and effectively structured piece of writing.
- I can use a wide range of well-selected sentence types and structures and precise vocabulary for impact.
- I can spell, punctuate and use grammar accurately so that writing is virtually error free.

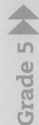

Grade 5

- I can communicate effectively and hold my reader's interest.
- I can produce a well-structured and purposeful piece of writing.
- I can vary my sentence types and structures and use vocabulary for effect.
- I can spell, punctuate and use grammar accurately with occasional errors.

Grade 2

- I can communicate simply in English with some clarity for my reader.
- I can produce writing with a basic structure and some awareness of purpose.
- I can show some control over sentences and use familiar vocabulary.
- I can spell, punctuate and use grammar with a little accuracy.

Introducing language skills

You are learning to:
- understand some basic language subject terminology
- examine and analyse language
- think about why language is used in certain ways and how it might affect you.

Testing: AO2
For: Paper 1 Question 2

1 Getting you thinking

Some of your first uses of the English language may have been the names of things around you. A baby's first words, for example, are often 'teddy', 'ball' and 'cup'. This is how you learn to make sense of the world, by labelling and naming the things you see.

The words that do the job of labelling and naming are called **nouns**. You can always test to see if a word is a noun by putting a determiner in front of it. The most common determiners are **a, an**, and **the**.

As you developed your language skills, you probably needed to be able to recognise and describe more specific things – you may have needed to ask for your brown teddy rather than a pink one; a football rather than a tennis ball; a clean cup rather than a dirty one.

The words that do the job of describing nouns are called **adjectives**.

a Organise the following words into two columns headed **Noun** and **Adjective**.

> black house web silvery chilly door torrential
> wispy cat moon haunted breeze rain creaking

b Now look at your lists of nouns and adjectives. Pair up each noun with the most appropriate adjective from the list. An example has been done for you below.

haunted house

If you add a determiner to this pairing, you create a **noun phrase**.

the haunted house – a haunted house

Go on to create **noun phrases** from all of your pairings by adding 'a' or 'the'.

c Look again at the **noun phrases** you have created. What type of story might you be reading if you found these noun phrases in it? Can you explain why?

② Explore the skills

Now look at what happens if you change the adjective in a noun phrase.

- a lonely house
- a summer house

When writers add an adjective, they are sharpening the mental picture for you, the reader. This is known as **modification**.

a Look at these noun phrases below. How does each one change the mental picture you have of a house? Jot down what you see in your mind's eye for each one.

- a newly built house
- an imposing house
- a dilapidated house
- a seaside house
- the family house

b Write your own list of noun phrases using the following nouns:

- night
- sky

Key term

modification: changing the impression or image of something by changing the word or words that describe it

(c) Look at this extract from a poem called 'Off course' in which the writer uses noun phrases to describe a space mission.

the turning continents the space debris

the golden lifeline the space walk

the crawling deltas the camera moon

the pitch velvet the rough sleep

the crackling headphone the space silence

         Edwin Morgan, 'Off course'

Choose four of the noun phrases and write down what you see in your mind's eye.

(d) Now imagine you are on the space mission in the poem and replace all of the adjectives in your four chosen noun phrases with ideas of your own. How does this **modification** change what you might see in your mind's eye?

For example:

the turning continents ⟶ the distant continents

③ Develop the skills

Your choice of **verbs** and **adverbs** can also help to create a more specific picture for your reader.

Making an interesting choice of **verb** can add movement, action and states of being to the picture that is created.

An **adverb** adds to this by giving details about how the action is taking place.

(a) Read this extract from Ray Bradbury's novel *Dandelion Wine* where the interesting verbs have been highlighted for you.

Key terms

verbs: actions or doing words that are the driving force of the sentence. They can show movement, action, states of being, and can also communicate when things are happening, depending on their tense, for example, past, present, future

adverbs: words that modify verbs to describe how something is being done

The grass whispered under his body. He put his arm down, feeling the sheath of fuzz on it, and far away, below, his toes creaking in his shoes. The wind sighed over his shelled ears. The world slipped bright over the glassy rounds of his eyeballs like images sparked in a crystal sphere. Flowers were sun and fiery spots of sky strewn through the woodland.

         Ray Bradbury, from *Dandelion Wine*

b Take each verb in the passage and add two different adverbs to it. For example:

The grass whispered softly

The grass whispered stealthily

c Then annotate each of your pairings with the different impressions they create. For example:

The grass whispered softly – suggests a summer day/ something or somewhere pleasant – a gentle breeze.
The grass whispered stealthily – has a sense of unease, sounds like an unwelcoming place. There is tension.

4 Final task

a Read the extract from *Dandelion Wine* again. It describes a boy lying in grass in summer. Plan your response to the following examination task by selecting two interesting noun phrases and two interesting verbs and annotating them with your impressions.

How does the writer use language here to describe the boy's response to the beautiful summer's day?

The grass whispered under his body. He put his arm down, feeling the sheath of fuzz on it, and far away, below, his toes creaking in his shoes. The wind sighed over his shelled ears. The world slipped bright over the glassy rounds of his eyeballs like images sparked in a crystal sphere. Flowers were sun and fiery spots
5 of sky strewn through the woodland. Birds flickered like skipped stones across the vast inverted pond of heaven. His breath raked over his teeth, going in ice, coming out fire. Insects shocked the air with electric clearness. Ten thousand individual hairs grew a millionth of an inch on his head. He heard the twin hearts beating in each ear, the third heart beating in his throat, the two hearts throbbing
10 in his wrists, the real heart pounding in his chest. The million pores on his body opened.
I'm *really* alive! he thought. I never knew it before, or if I did I don't remember!

b Write up your response.

Developing language skills

You are learning to:
- understand some more creative language subject terminology
- examine and analyse language in fiction texts
- think about why writers use language in certain ways and how it might affect you.

Testing: AO2
For: Paper 1 Question 2

1 Getting you thinking

As well as using specific words and phrases to create a picture for a reader, effective writers can also combine words and phrases to create different 'special effects' in their work. You can do this in your own writing for Paper 1 Question 5 too.

a Look again at the way Ray Bradbury described the flowers and the birds in the extract from *Dandelion Wine*:

> Flowers were sun and fiery spots of sky strewn through the woodland.
>
> Birds flickered like skipped stones across the vast inverted pond of heaven.

b If you imagine the flowers in the woodland, what colours do you see in your mind's eye and why?

c What activity is Bradbury reminding you of when he describes the movement of the birds? What does this suggest about the way the birds were moving?

By describing the flowers as sun and fire, Bradbury is using a **metaphor**.

By comparing the birds to skimming stones, Bradbury is using a **simile**.

2 Explore the skills

a In the grid on the following page, there are definitions of some of the special effects writers use. An example has been given describing aspects of summer. Complete a further example of your own describing aspects of winter.

Language special effect	Definition	Example: describing summer	Example: describing winter
metaphor	A way of creating an image of something by describing it as actually being something else.	The sun was a golden ball of fire in the mid-afternoon sky.	
simile	A way of creating an image of something by comparing it to something else using 'like' or 'as'.	The sky was as blue as a precious sapphire.	
personification	A way of describing something that isn't human by giving it the qualities of a human.	The sunflowers danced and nodded in the soft breeze.	
alliteration	A pattern of sounds in a description created by using words that begin with the same letter.	Sunshine sparkled on the silvery stream.	
onomatopoeia	A sound effect where you use a word to represent the noise you want to describe.	Parents sloshed and slapped sun cream on their wriggling toddlers.	

3 Develop the skills

a Read this extract from the novel *The God of Small Things* by Arundhati Roy. Think about the variety of language special effects she has used.

> May in Ayemenem is a hot, brooding month. The days are long and humid. The river shrinks and black crows gorge on bright mangoes in still, dustgreen trees. Red bananas ripen. Jackfruits burst. Dissolute bluebottles hum vacuously in the fruity air. Then they stun themselves against clear windowpanes and die, fatly baffled in the sun.
>
> [...]
>
> But by early June the south-west monsoon breaks and there are three months of wind and water with short spells of sharp, glittering sunshine that thrilled children snatch to play with.
>
> Arundhati Roy, from *The God of Small Things*

b Now consider the impact of the special effects.

- How is June different to May in the extract? What different impressions do you get from the **noun phrases**: 'hot, brooding month', 'sharp, glittering sunshine'?

- Which letter sound do you think has been repeated most in the first paragraph? What impression does this give of the season? How does Roy use **alliteration** to make a contrast in the second paragraph?

- What impression is given by the **verbs** 'gorge', 'ripen', 'burst'?

- Which two contrasting words give the impression of the sounds the bluebottles make?

- What do you imagine when you see the bluebottles described as 'fatly baffled'?

c Look at the response that Student A has made to this examination task.

How does the writer use language here to describe summer in Ayemenem?

The writer describes summer by telling us about May and June and how they are different. They use words such as 'hot' and 'humid'. The writer gives us lots of details about the place and tells us a lot about the different fruits. It sounds like the flies are drunk. June is very rainy as it is described as 'three months of wind and water'. The children like playing in it.

- Does the student tell us mainly about language or mainly about the content of the extract?
- Does the student use any terminology to identify features of language in the extract?
- Once they identify some words, is there anything to show the examiner what they understand about how the writer uses language?

d Now look at Student B's work in approaching the same question.

The writer shows how summer is changeable in Ayemenem by describing May using the noun phrase 'hot brooding month' and June as having 'sharp, glittering sunshine.' May sounds uncomfortable and oppressive but June seems bright and sparkling by comparison. This is reflected in the alliteration of 'short spells of sharp...sunshine' which sounds crisp and bright compared to the dull sound of the 'black crows' and 'bluebottles' in May. Things sound ugly and unhealthy in May through the use of interesting verbs such as 'gorge', 'ripen', 'burst' which makes me imagine greediness — like everything is too much. The onomatopoeia of 'hum' and 'stun' creates a disturbing image of the flies dying compared to the image of the 'thrilled children' playing in the healthier sunshine between the showers.

Look at the areas highlighted in yellow.

- What do you notice about how the student uses the correct terms?
- What has the student put in quotation marks?

Look at the comments highlighted in green.

- What is the student doing here in terms of thinking about the language used?
- What is this showing to the examiner marking their work?

In order to be successful, Student B has:

- clearly identified a number of interesting language features in the text
- given examples of each, correctly set out and punctuated
- commented on how they, as a reader, have responded to those language features.

④ Final task

a Read this next extract from *The God of Small Things* by Arundhati Roy.

> It was raining when Rahel came back to Ayemenem. Slanting silver ropes slammed into loose earth, ploughing it up like gunfire. The old house on the hill wore its steep, gabled roof pulled over its ears like a low hat. The walls, streaked with moss, had grown soft, and bulged a little with dampness that seeped up from the ground.
> 5 The wild, overgrown garden was full of the whisper and scurry of small lives. In the undergrowth a rat snake rubbed itself against a glistening stone.

b Using the successful method from Student B as your guide, plan and then write up this examination task for yourself:

How does the writer use language here to describe the place in the extract?

Checklist for success

- Identify a number of interesting language features in the text (2–3 will be fine).
- Give examples of each from the extract ensuring you use quotation marks.
- Think about how you have responded to those language features and write a comment explaining what they make *you* think about, feel or imagine.

Exam tip

When writing about the language features a writer uses, try not to make general comments like 'it makes the reader read on' or 'it keeps them hooked'. Explain what you can see in your imagination when you read that language feature or technique. Explain what you see, think or feel.

Applying language skills to Paper 1 Question 2

You are learning to:
- understand how the examination question and mark scheme works
- practise your skills in finding features in a fiction text
- think about a method for answering a task
- apply the mark scheme to student responses.

Testing: AO2
For: Paper 1 Question 2

1 Getting you thinking

a Look at the wording of the examination task for Paper 1, Question 2. You will be asked to answer about language.

Look in detail at this extract from **lines 8 to 18** of the source:

How does the writer use language here to describe…?

You could include the writer's choice of:

- words and phrases

- language features and techniques

- sentence forms.

(8 marks)

The source material will be printed in your question paper. For Question 2 you will only be asked to work with a short extract. This extract will have been specially picked to contain lots of interesting aspects of language.

Here you will be given a specific focus or topic.

Note here, the question says 'could' and not 'must'. This is just to help you focus on language. You don't need to write about all of these aspects.

Here the examiner is suggesting you could include ideas on interesting single words, like adjectives or verbs and interesting phrases like noun phrases and verbs with adverbs.

Here the examiner is suggesting you could comment on specific features like similes or metaphors, or techniques such as **pathetic fallacy**.

Here the examiner is suggesting you could comment on how sentences are used for effect – such as an exclamation or a rhetorical question.

There are 8 marks for the task. You will only have around 10–12 minutes to answer it. You are not expected to write an essay. Pick no more than three aspects to work with.

2 Explore the skills

a Look at this extract from the mark scheme.

- Level 2 will show **'some'** understanding and make **an attempt**
- Level 3 will be **clear**, focused and on the task
- Level 4 will be **detailed** with some insightful and **perceptive** comments.

Key term

pathetic fallacy: where a writer uses the description of the natural world to reflect the mood or atmosphere in the story. For example, a rainy, gloomy day as a background for a character who is unhappy or depressed

Level 4 Detailed, perceptive **7–8 marks**	Shows detailed and perceptive understanding of language: • Analyses the effects of language • Selects a judicious range of textual detail • Makes sophisticated and accurate use of subject terminology
Level 3 Clear, relevant **5–6 marks**	Shows clear understanding of language: • Explains clearly the effects of language • Selects a range of relevant detail • Makes clear and accurate use of subject terminology
Level 2 Some, attempts **3–4 marks**	Shows some understanding of language: • Attempts to comment on the effect of language • Selects some appropriate textual detail • Makes some use of subject terminology

Now look carefully at the ladder of skills on the left – begin on the bottom rung.

- The examiner is looking for you to use subject terminology to describe what you find in the text, for example, noun phrase, adverb, simile, personification.

- Then they are looking for you to give an example of what you have found. If you can do this, you will achieve the lower mark in the band.

- However, if you are able to comment on the effect of the language you have found you will earn the higher mark in the band.

b Read this extract from Daphne du Maurier's novel *Rebecca* where the central character dreams of returning to her former home, 'Manderley' – a huge, imposing house full of dark secrets.

The drive wound away in front of me, twisting and turning as it had always done, but as I advanced I was aware that a change had come upon it; it was narrow and unkept, not the drive that we had known. At first I was puzzled and did not understand, and it was only when I bent my head to avoid the low swinging branch of a tree that I realized what had happened. Nature had come into her own again and, little by little, in her stealthy, insidious way had encroached upon the drive with long, tenacious fingers. The woods, always a menace even in the past, had triumphed in the end. They crowded, dark and uncontrolled, to the borders of the drive. The beeches with white, naked limbs leant close to one another, their branches intermingled in a strange embrace, making a vault above my head like the archway of a church.

Daphne du Maurier, from *Rebecca*

c Make a copy of the table below. For each language feature, find an example from the text.

Language feature	Example
alliteration	
personification	
noun phrases	
simile	

③ Develop the skills

To achieve the highest marks in each level, you need to be able to comment meaningfully on the effect of language. But what does this mean?

a Look at this response from a student and make notes on the questions.

Student A

> The writer uses alliteration in the extract, for example, 'twisting and turning' to describe the drive. This makes it stick in the reader's mind and makes them want to read on.

What does Student A's comment on effect actually mean?

Is it specifically about what is in this text or could it apply to any text?

b Now read the following response. This answer shows features of Level 3 achievement.

Student B

> The writer uses alliteration in the extract to describe the drive as 'twisting and turning.' This creates an image of a mysterious place and also makes me imagine somewhere grand. It makes you feel as though you might get lost there and the repeated 't' sounds are sharp, sound unwelcoming and perhaps a little scary.

- What do you notice about the way this student has dealt with effect?

- Have they written about readers in general or the effect on themselves?

- What key words have they used instead of 'effect' in their comment?

(c) Go back to the examples of the language features you found earlier. Select three. Write up three paragraphs following the method that Student B used.

(4) Final task

Using the mark scheme grid in **Explore the skills**, decide on a mark for these students who have completed the task set in Week 7, Lesson 2. Write a comment, giving reasons for your decision.

Student A

> Roy uses alliteration to describe the rain as 'slanting silver ropes'. The repeated 's' sounds make the rain sound sharp and creates an image of something hard and metallic. The house is personified as having its roof 'pulled over its ears like a low hat.' This makes me imagine an older house, hunkering down into the landscape. 'The whisper and scurry of small lives' is a metaphor for all of the tiny hidden creatures in the wild garden and helps us to imagine how small and busy they are even in the harsh weather.

Student B

> There is some alliteration in the text 'slanting silver'. This is very catchy and makes it memorable for the reader. There is also a simile 'pulled over its ears like a low hat'. The writer uses adjectives like 'old' to describe the house and 'wild' to describe the garden. This makes me picture it in my mind.

Exam tip

When commenting on language, always ask yourself these questions about the examples you have chosen:

- What does this phrase/ feature make me think of?

- What am I imagining in my mind's eye?

- What feeling do these words/images give me?

In this way, you will always have something specific to say about the examples you use.

Applying language skills to Paper 1 Question 2

You are learning to:
- practise an examination task, step by step
- think about the mark scheme skills
- develop your ability to comment on effect
- evaluate your answer.

Testing: AO2
For: Paper 1 Question 2

1 Getting you thinking

a Look at this examination task. Then read the extract below in which the narrator leaves his countryside home in 1934 to seek a better, more exciting future.

How does the writer use language here to describe the narrator's reasons for leaving home?

As I left home that morning and walked away from the sleeping village, it never occurred to me that others had done this before me.

I was propelled, of course, by the traditional forces that had sent many generations along this road – by the small tight valley closing in around one, stifling the breath with its mossy mouth, the cottage walls narrowing like the arms of an iron maiden, the local girls whispering, 'Marry, and settle down.' Months of restless unease, leading to this inevitable moment, had been spent wandering about the hills, mournfully whistling, and watching the high open fields stepping away eastwards under gigantic clouds…

Laurie Lee, from *As I Walked Out One Midsummer Morning*

Exam tip

This is a challenging passage, but if you do face something in the examination that you are unsure about or find difficult: stop, think and apply the method you have been working on. Tackle the passage step by step.

② Explore the skills

a First of all, remind yourself of the mark scheme.

What three skills is the examiner looking for you to show? Note them down in the order they should appear in each section of your response.

Remember the notion of 'climbing the ladder' and use this extract from the mark scheme to help you.

Level 3 Clear, relevant **5–6 marks**	Shows clear understanding of language: <ul><li>Explains clearly the effects of language</li><li>Selects a range of relevant textual detail</li><li>Makes clear and accurate use of terminology</li></ul>

b Now collect some of the language features and language 'special effects' in the extract.

Remember, you will only be writing about approximately three aspects of language at most in the time you have.

1. noun phrases: the sleeping village, the small tight valley, the high open fields, gigantic clouds
2. interesting verbs:
3. verbs + adverbs:
4. personification:
5. simile:

c Select three of your chosen aspects of language to work with in the next activity.

③ Develop the skills

Now you have enough material to address the lower order skills of the mark scheme: the first two rungs of the ladder.

You are now going to move on to think about the higher order skill: commenting on effect.

Even though this passage is challenging, do not be tempted to slip into making generalised and meaningless comments just to be able to say 'something' about the language. **Stop and think** about the method.

- What does this phrase/feature make me think of?
- What am I imagining in my mind's eye?
- What feeling do these words/images give me?

a Look at these images suggested by the noun phrases
collected above:

the sleeping village

the small tight valley

the high open fields

gigantic clouds

b Make some notes on the following:

- What do you see in each picture?

- What feeling or atmosphere does each picture suggest?

- How do they help you to understand the scene Laurie
  Lee is describing?

- Can you 'see' the *effect* the writer is trying to create by
  using the phrases?

c Annotate each of your chosen language features with
what each one makes you think of, imagine or feel. Try
to visualise what is being described in your mind's eye.
This will form the basis of your more specific comments
on effect.

(d) You are now going to take all of the notes and ideas you have collected:

- your aspects of language
- your examples
- your notes on effect

and put them together into an examination answer. Aim to write up your ideas in no more than 8–10 minutes. Remember, this is *not* an essay task. It is a short answer, 8-mark task.

(e) Look back at the mark scheme and example answers in Week 8, Lesson 1 and decide whether your work could be described as:

- an attempt
- clear and relevant
- perceptive and detailed

by thinking:

- is my work similar to Student B or stronger
- is my work similar to Student A or stronger?

(4) Final task

(a) Complete this final task, working independently, in no more than 15 minutes. Use the method you have practised.

How does the writer use language here to describe the way he is feeling at this point in his journey?

That first day alone – and now I was really alone at last – steadily declined in excitement and vigour. As I tramped through the dust towards the Wiltshire Downs a growing reluctance weighed me down. White elder-blossom and dog-roses hung in the hedges, blank as unwritten paper, and the hot empty road – there were few motor cars then – reflected Sunday's waste
5 and indifference. High sulky summer sucked me towards it, and I offered no resistance at all. Through the solitary morning and afternoon I found myself longing for some opposition or rescue, for the sound of hurrying footsteps coming after me and family voices calling me back.

(b) When you have finished, check your answer against the mark scheme and student examples in Week 8, Lesson 1.

Checklist for success

- Select no more than three language ideas or special effects.
- Make sure you give an example of each one.
- Make a comment that explains its effect by deciding on what it makes you think of, feel or imagine.

Introducing structural features

You are learning to:
- understand some of the basic ways writers structure and sequence their work
- develop your knowledge of subject terminology
- recognise how structural features are used to make a particular impression on you
- practise a structure question.

Testing: AO2
For: Paper 1 Question 3

 Getting you thinking

Once you've considered the language clues the writer has left you, you should also consider the **structure** of the text. Often we think that texts are just organised into paragraphs.

The structure of a text, however, includes **all** of the ways in which it has been 'built' and put together by the writer for effect. You might think of structure as being like the building blocks of a text.

The ways in which a writer chooses to organise a text may include:
- the **narrative perspective** (for example, first person or third person)
- the paragraphing
- the order of ideas or topics
- chronology (sequencing of events)
- the sentence structure
- the pace at which the story seems to move (for example, fast and dramatic, or slow paced and gradually unfolding)
- the use of time or tense in a story (for example, present or past)
- the patterns or structural 'special effects' within the writing such as repetition, listing and contrast.

Key term

narrative perspective: the point of view from which a story is told

Asking yourself why the writer made the decisions to structure the piece as they have will help you to build your examination answer effectively.

 Look at how this extract is put together or **structured**.

> In the flat upstairs, an old man is looking for a box of matches to light the gas under the kettle, he turns to the table and he sees an envelope lying there, his name scratched across it in wavering handwriting. He smiles, he turns and opens the cutlery drawer of the Welsh dresser, he takes out an envelope with his wife's name on it, his own handwriting as newly unreliable as hers.
>
> He places the two cards side by side, he thinks about opening his for a moment and decides not to. He looks for the matches and thinks about that day.
>
> Jon McGregor, from *If Nobody Speaks of Remarkable Things*

b What special event do you think the old man in the extract is celebrating? When might a husband and wife send a card to each other?

c How does the **structure** of the text help you to work this out?

- What tense is used?
- Is this happening in the past or present?
- Why are there only two paragraphs?
- Is there a fast pace here, or a slow pace?
- What is it about the sentences that creates the pace?
- Think about the sequence of events with the cards and why he waits to open his card.

d Look closely at the final sentence. It is a **compound sentence** joining two ideas together. What two ideas are joined? What is implied by 'that day'.

e The final sentence gives the writer the opportunity to create a 'story within the story'. Where do you think the story could go next?

> **Key term**
>
> **compound sentence:** when two ideas (which could be simple sentences) are joined together. They are joined with conjunctions such as for, and, nor, but, or, yet, so

② Explore the skills

a Now read the next extract from the same novel.

It wasn't a spectacular wedding. It happened in a hurry, and they only spent one night together before he went away again, went away properly.

[…]

But it was a wedding, and they looked each other in the eyes and said the words, they made their vows and they have kept them all these years.

[…]

And they took the wedding certificate back to their new house, propped it up on the chest of drawers at the foot of the bed, and spent the whole evening looking at it.

[…]

She said, tell me the story of us, tell me it the way you'll tell our children, when they ask.

[…]

And he'd always say it the same way, starting with once upon a time there was a handsome soldier boy with a smart uniform…

b A student has made the following notes on the key structural features of the extract.

Add your own ideas to these in note form, exploring the impact of the features on the meaning and thinking about what they help the writer to communicate to you.

- starts with a simple sentence – seems to be the only one
- tense changes
- loads of paragraphs here
- there's speech in it but no speech marks – indirect
- another of those 'story within a story' things
- his story tells me what time in history this is and why he's leaving because…

③ Develop the skills

You know now that the following structural features are important in this text:

- past and present
- paragraph structure
- sentence structure
- story within a story
- indirect speech.

a Using a copy of this final extract, identify and annotate for yourself the structural features that make an impact on the meaning of the story.

And that first time he'd told the story, that night, lying side by side on the bed, fully clothed, neither of them said anything when he finished, they just lay there looking at the official type, the formal words.

And she'd whispered it's a good story isn't it? And the last thing she'd said to him,
5 just before she went to sleep that night, quietly, almost as though she thought he was asleep, she said you will come back won't you, you will keep safe, please, you will come home?

b Look again at the extract you read in **Explore the skills.**

- What do you now know about the young soldier in the final extract?
- What do you know about the marriage that took place?
- What has Jon McGregor managed to communicate to you about the relationship between the old man and his wife through his interesting structure?

4 Final task

a Using the notes and ideas you have gathered, write 250–300 words in response to the following task.

> **How has the writer used interesting structural features for this story to show us more about the elderly man and his relationship with his wife?**

You could begin:

> Jon McGregor adds interest through the structural choices he makes in the extract. For example, the use of time is important. He begins by using a setting in the present, where we see an elderly man, who is pleased to see his wife has remembered their wedding anniversary. He emphasises that this is happening 'now' by using the present tense, for example...

Checklist for success

- Think about how Jon McGregor's **structural choices** have helped you to understand and realise more about the elderly man and his relationship with his wife.
- Aim to include **two to three separate structural features** and explore how they help us to understand the meaning of the text and add interest.

Developing skills with structure

You are learning to:
- understand some of the more creative ways writers can use structural features in a text
- develop your knowledge of subject terminology
- develop your skills in commenting on the effect of structural features.

Testing: AO2
For: Paper 1 Question 3

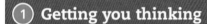

① Getting you thinking

Within sentences themselves, writers can create different patterns to help you feel a particular effect. They also vary their choice of sentence length and structure to change the pace of the text.

a Read this extract from Jon McGregor's novel *If Nobody Speaks of Remarkable Things* where the writer is describing a city at night.

> So listen.
>
> Listen, and there is more to hear.
>
> The rattle of a dustbin lid knocked to the floor.
>
> The scrawl and scratch of two hackle-raised cats.
>
> The sudden thundercrash of bottles emptied into crates. The slam-slam of car doors, the changing of gears, the hobbled clip-clop of a slow walk home. The rippled roll of shutters pulled down on late-night cafes, a crackled voice crying street names for taxis, a loud scream that lingers and cracks into laughter, a bang that might just be an old car backfiring, a callbox calling out for an answer, a treeful of birds tricked into morning, a whistle and a shout and a broken glass, a blare of soft music and a blam of hard beats, a barking and yelling and singing and crying and it all swells up all the rumbles and crashes and bangings and slams, all the noise and the rush and the non-stop wonder of the song of the city you can hear if you listen the song and it stops in some rare and sacred dead time, sandwiched between the late sleepers and the early risers, there is a miracle of silence.
>
> Everything has stopped.
>
> Jon McGregor, from *If Nobody Speaks of Remarkable Things*

b Add an example from the extract to the table below, which has definitions of some of the more common structural special effects writers use.

Structural feature	Definition	Example from the extract
minor sentence	An incomplete sentence that doesn't contain a main verb.	
listing	Where a number of different items or images are linked together or sequenced with commas to build up a picture or impression.	
repetition	Where the same word or phrase is used more than once for emphasis or exaggeration.	
simple sentence	A sentence that contains one clear-cut idea and one verb or action.	

② Explore the skills

You are now going to 'zoom in' on the unusual structural effects of this text. Look at each of the extracts below and make notes of the questions that accompany them.

Key term

....

minor sentence: a sentence that lacks one or more of the elements that go to make up a full sentence, for example, a subject or a main verb

The rattle of a dustbin lid knocked to the floor.

The scrawl and scratch of two hackle-raised cats.

The sudden thundercrash of bottles emptied into crates.

a What is unusual about each of these sentences? Who is 'doing' the action in each case?

The rippled roll of shutters pulled down on late-night cafes, a crackled voice crying street names for taxis, a loud scream that lingers and cracks into laughter, a bang that might just be an old car backfiring, a callbox calling out for an answer, a treeful of birds tricked into morning, a whistle and a shout and a broken glass, a blare of soft music and a blam of hard beats, a barking and yelling and singing and crying and it all swells up all the rumbles and crashes and bangings and slams, all the noise and the rush and the non-stop wonder of the song of the city you can hear if you listen the song

b Is this a sentence? Why/why not? What effect is the writer trying to create here? Rather than using visual images like similes, what does the writer do? Why is this an effective choice for describing the night in the city?

> a barking and yelling and singing and crying and it all swells up all the rumbles and crashes and bangings and slams, all the noise and the rush and the non-stop wonder of the song of the city you can hear if you listen the song and it stops in some rare and sacred dead time, sandwiched between the late sleepers and the early risers, there is a miracle of silence.
>
> Everything has stopped.

c How does the writer bring you to a halt in your reading? Why does he change the pace here? What time do you think he means by 'the miracle of silence'? How does he 'show' the silence in the way he has shaped the text here? What would you say is the impact of the simple sentence at the end?

③ Develop the skills

When thinking about the effect of a structural feature, always ask yourself: What does this feature make me think of, imagine and feel? However, you should also question what the **structural feature** is actually *doing* to the text itself. Think about the possibilities by studying the diagram below.

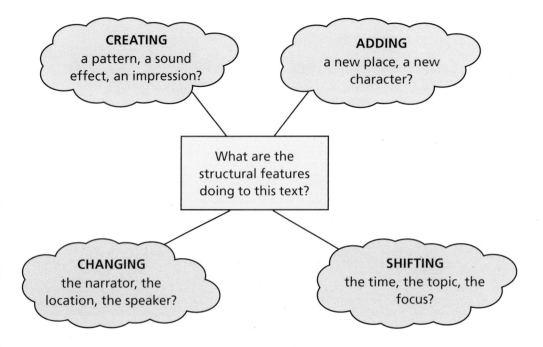

a Look back at the four examples of structural features that you collected in **Explore the skills**. Write a comment for each one, suggesting what the feature does to the text and the effect this has on you, the reader. Use the thought bubbles on the previous page to help you add ideas to the method.

- What does this feature make me think of?
- What am I imagining in my mind's eye?
- What feeling do these words/images give me?

4 Final task

a Look at this opening to a student response to the task:

> **How has the writer structured the extract from *If Nobody Speaks of Remarkable Things* to interest you as a reader?**

The extract begins with the repetition of the word 'listen'. ———— structural feature / example

It shifts the focus of the extract onto the sounds, which ———— what the feature does to the text

McGregor uses to build up his description of the city at night. This creates the feeling that we as readers should ———— the effect on us: what we think/feel/imagine

be paying attention to the sounds of the city, not just to what it looks like. This is effective if we think about the fact this is about the night time. We are encouraged to think about what we hear through the darkness, not what we see.

b Choose two more structural features that you have worked on and continue the response, following the method in the annotations.

Applying skills with structure to Paper 1 Question 3

You are learning to:
- understand how the examination question and mark scheme works for the structure question
- practise your skills in finding structural features in a fiction text
- think about a method for answering a task
- plan and write your own response.

Testing: AO2
For: Paper 1 Question 3

1 Getting you thinking

a Take a few minutes to think in more detail about the type of examination task you will be asked to answer about language. The notes will help you to understand the task thoroughly.

You now need to think about the **whole** of the source.

> This means you are able to take ideas about structure from anywhere in the text. It does not mean you have to write about everything in the text or every aspect of its structure.

The text is from...

> Look for clues here. It will tell you if it's from an opening or the middle of a text, for example.

How has the writer structured the text to interest you as a reader?

> The 'How' part means you need to identify aspects of structure. The reference to 'interest' means write about the effect on you as a reader.

You could write about:

> Again, note this says 'could' and not 'must'. The bullet points are suggestions to keep you on track.

- what the writer focuses your attention on at the beginning

> Think about narrative perspective, who we meet and location.

- how and why the writer changes the focus as the source develops

> Here you might be thinking about topic shifts in the paragraphs, changes in place, new characters being introduced, shifts in the time or tense.

- any other structural features that interest you

> Here is where you might 'zoom in' on patterns in the sentences or sentence structures – the structural 'special effects'.

(8 marks)

> Again, this is a low tariff question. It is a short answer, not an essay.

Exam tip

The bullet points in this task invite you to ask key questions about the text. When you are faced with an unseen text in the exam, it is important to be able to **ask questions** yourself, before you can answer the exam questions properly.

2 Explore the skills

For Paper 1 Question 3, the way a writer has **structured** a text can help us to 'solve' problems in understanding the text and piece together its meaning like a jigsaw puzzle.

a Look at the diagram below.

Whose views?
Who is telling the story? What *perspective* is it from?

What time is it?
How is time ordered in it? What sort of *sequence* do I see?

Where am I?
What's the place, location, *setting*? How did I find out?

Who is here?
What *character*(s) have I met and how were they introduced?

What's it made of?
What shapes, styles and patterns can I see in the sentences?

b Now read this extract from the opening of *The Girl with the Dragon Tattoo*. Use the structure jigsaw to make your own notes on *how* the writer has structured the text.

It happened every year, was almost a ritual. And this was his eighty-second birthday. When, as usual, the flower was delivered, he took off the wrapping paper and then picked up the telephone to call Detective Superintendent Morrell who, when he retired, had moved to Lake Siljan in Dalarna. They were not only the same age, they had been born on the same day – which was something of an irony under the circumstances. The old policeman was sitting with his coffee, waiting, expecting the call.

'It arrived.'

'What is it this year?'

'I don't know what kind it is. It's white.'

'No letter, I suppose.'

'Just the flower.' [...]

'Postmark?'

'Stockholm.'

'Handwriting?'

'Same as always, all in capitals. Upright, neat lettering.'

With that, the subject was exhausted, and not another word was exchanged for almost a minute. The retired policeman leaned back in his chair and drew on his pipe. He knew he was no longer expected to come up with a pithy comment or any sharp question which would shed a new light on the case. Those days had long since past. [...]

The policeman was a hardened veteran. [...] During his career he had brought in poachers, wife beaters, con men, car thieves, and drunk drivers. He had dealt with burglars, drug dealers, rapists, and one deranged bomber. [...] All in all he could look back on an impressive career.

He was anything but pleased.

For the detective, the 'Case of the Pressed Flowers' had been nagging at him for years – his last, unsolved and frustrating case. The situation was doubly absurd because after spending literally thousands of hours brooding, on duty and off, he could not say beyond doubt that a crime had indeed been committed.

After putting down the telephone the eighty-two-year-old birthday boy sat for a long time looking at the pretty but meaningless flower whose name he did not yet know. Then he looked up to the wall above his desk. There hung forty-three pressed flowers in their frames. [...]

Without warning he began to weep. He surprised himself with this sudden burst of emotion after almost forty years.

Stieg Larsson, from *The Girl with the Dragon Tattoo*

c Now take a close look at this extract from the mark scheme for Question 3.

Level 3 Clear, relevant 5–6 marks	Shows clear understanding of structural features: • Explains clearly the effects of structural features • Selects a range of relevant examples • Makes clear and accurate use of subject terminology
Level 2 Some, attempts 3–4 marks	Shows some understanding of structural features: • Attempts to comment on the effect of structural features • Selects some appropriate examples • Makes some use of subject terminology
Level 1 Simple, limited 1–2 marks	Shows simple awareness of structural features: • Offers simple comment on effect • Selects simple references or examples • Makes simple use of subject terminology, not always appropriately

Look carefully at the ladder of skills above – begin on the bottom rung. You could use the framework below to help you:

- The examiner is looking for me to use…

- Then they are looking for me to…

- I should then go on to offer a…

d Using the mark scheme above, decide which level the following response should be placed in, what mark you would give it and why. Use the notes in the annotations to help you.

> This extract starts off by introducing an old man, opening presents on his birthday. It seems unusual as he phones the police about his presents. The writer organises the extract into paragraphs. These follow on nicely from each other and give a sequence to the text. There is some talking in it and the writer sets all the talking out neatly so the reader knows who is talking and doesn't get muddled up. All in all this is a very well structured story and leaves me wanting to know more.

Is this about structure or content?

Is there anything else to say here? What has the student not noticed about the sequence of paragraphs and about whose views we are getting?

Is this specific or general?

Does this show knowledge of subject terminology?

Is this adding to the marks or not?

Exam tip

You can give examples of things like simple sentences, or repetition as quotations. However, your exam source will have its lines numbered for you. If you want to give examples of where a location changes, a new character is introduced or time changes, it's fine to say, 'On line 23, for example…' or 'We can see the shift on line 6…'

3 **Develop the skills**

Look again at your notes from **Explore the skills**. In the exam, you should aim to write about no more than three features. Question 3 is an 8-mark question and you will only have 8–10 minutes to work on this.

a Select the three structural features you feel most confident about.

b Organise your notes into a table like the one below.

c Reflect on your work from Week 9, Lesson 2 to help you comment meaningfully on the effect of the features.

Structural feature	Where to find the example (quotations or line numbers are fine)	What the feature is *doing* to the text (creating/ adding/ changing/ shifting)	What the effect or impact is on me (think/ imagine/feel)
1.			
2.			
3.			

④ Final task

Now take all of the notes and ideas you have gathered, your:

- aspects of structure
- examples
- notes on effect

and put them together to answer this examination task.

You now need to think about the *whole* of the extract from the opening of the novel *The Girl with the Dragon Tattoo* provided earlier.

How has the writer structured the text to interest you as a reader?

You could write about:

- what the writer focuses your attention on at the beginning
- how and why the writer changes the focus as the source develops
- any other structural features that interest you.

Aim to write up your ideas in no more than 8–10 minutes.

Applying skills with structure to Paper 1 Question 3

You are learning to:
- practise an examination task, step by step
- think about the mark scheme skills
- develop your ability to plan your response
- develop your ability to comment on the effect of the structural features
- evaluate your answer against other student responses.

Testing: AO2
For: Paper 1 Question 3

1 Getting you thinking

a You are now going to work, step by step, through a Question 3 task.

Look at this examination task and then carefully read the extract below.

You now need to think about the **whole** of the source.

The text is from the opening of *As I Walked Out One Midsummer Morning* by Laurie Lee.

How has the writer structured the text to interest you as a reader?

You could write about:

- what the writer focuses your attention on at the beginning

- how and why the writer changes the focus as the source develops

- any other structural features that interest you.

(8 marks)

As I left home that morning and walked away from the sleeping village, it never occurred to me that others had done this before me.

I was propelled, of course, by the traditional forces that had sent many generations along this road – by the small tight valley closing in around one, stifling the
5 breath with its mossy mouth, the cottage walls narrowing like the arms of an iron maiden, the local girls whispering, 'Marry, and settle down.' Months of restless unease, leading to this inevitable moment, had been spent wandering about the hills, mournfully whistling, and watching the high open fields stepping away eastwards under gigantic clouds...

10 And now I was on my journey, in a pair of thick boots
and with a hazel stick in my hand. Naturally, I was going
to London, which lay a hundred miles to the east; and it
seemed equally obvious that I should go on foot. [...]

That first day alone – and now I was really alone at last –
15 steadily declined in excitement and vigour. As I tramped
through the dust towards the Wiltshire Downs a growing
reluctance weighed me down. White elder-blossom and
dog-roses hung in the hedges, blank as unwritten paper,
and the hot empty road – there were few motor cars then
20 – reflected Sunday's waste and indifference. High sulky
summer sucked me towards it, and I offered no resistance
at all. Through the solitary morning and afternoon I found
myself longing for some opposition or rescue, for the
sound of hurrying footsteps coming after me and family
25 voices calling me back.

None came. I was free. I was affronted by freedom. The
day's silence said, Go where you will. It's all yours. You
asked for it. It's up to you now. You're on your own and
nobody's going to stop you. As I walked, I was taunted
30 by echoes of home, by the tinkling sounds of the kitchen,
shafts of sun from the windows falling across the familiar
furniture, across the bedroom and the bed I had left. [...]

When darkness came, full of moths and beetles, I was
too weary to put up the tent. So I lay myself down in the
35 middle of a field and stared up at the brilliant stars. I was
oppressed by the velvety emptiness of the world and the
swathes of soft grass I lay on. Then the fumes of the night
finally put me to sleep – my first night without a roof or bed.

Laurie Lee, from *As I Walked Out One Midsummer Morning*

② Explore the skills

a First of all, remind yourself of the mark scheme in Week 10,
Lesson 1.

What three skills are the examiners looking for you to
show? Note them down in the order they should appear in
each section of your response.

Remember the notion of 'climbing the ladder' and use this
final extract from the mark scheme to help you.

Level 4 Perceptive, detailed 7–8 marks	Shows detailed and perceptive understanding of structure: • Analyses the effects of structural features • Selects a judicious range of examples • Makes sophisticated and accurate use of terminology

b Now carefully read the text again and collect some the structural features and structural 'special effects' in the extract.

Whose views?	Who is telling the story? Perspective?	
What time is it?	How is time ordered in the extract? What sort of sequence do I see?	Time spans the sequence of the whole day–begins morning and ends 'When darkness came'. There is past tense and past continuous tense 'I was going…'
Where am I?	What's the place, location, setting? How did I find out?	
Who is here?	What characters have I met and how were they introduced?	
What's it made of?	What shapes, styles, patterns can I see in the sentences?	

Think back

You could do this in a list or a table like the one here, which reflects the structure jigsaw from Week 10, Lesson 1.

Don't attempt to find an example of everything you have learned. Remember, you will only be writing about approximately three aspects of structure at the most in the time you have.

③ Develop the skills

a Decide which three aspects of structure you feel most confident in writing about.

You are now going to think about the higher order skill: commenting on effect.

b Write a comment for each of the three features you have decided on, suggesting what the feature **does to the text** and the effect this has on **you, the reader**.

Exam tip

Ask yourself these questions.

Is each feature:

creating?   adding?
changing?   shifting?

What does this feature make me:

think of?   imagine?
feel?

c Now take all of the notes and ideas you have gathered, your:

- aspects of structure
- examples
- notes on effect

and put them together to answer the task set in **Getting you thinking**. Aim to write up your ideas in no more than 10 minutes. Remember, this is not an essay task. It is a short answer, low mark tariff task.

④ Final task

Look back at the mark scheme and the example marked responses below. Decide whether your work could be described as:

- an attempt: Level 2
- clear and relevant: Level 3
- perceptive and detailed: Level 4

by thinking:

- is my work similar to Student A, weaker or stronger?
- is my work similar to Student B , weaker or stronger?

Student A

Laurie Lee structures his text in first person , 'I was on my journey', which makes it feel like the narrator is talking directly to you as a reader and telling you his story.

The extract also is organised in paragraphs which change with the time of day, for example he starts off 'that morning' and the extract ends 'when darkness came'. This is so the writer can give the impression of the whole day and how he is feeling.

Also, he uses past and present in the extract as he tells you he is heading to London in paragraph 3 but he also thinks back to his family home 'and the bed I had left'. This shows his feelings about his journey and it makes me feel he might be regretting setting off.

some terminology

examples

attempts a comment here – not totally explained.

another example

again, not fully explained but attempting a comment

All Level 2: 4 marks

Student B

The first person narrative perspective of the text gives it an immediate feel as though the narrator is relating his experiences to the reader as an anecdote. This is also emphasised through the sentence structure, which is filled with pauses like a conversation (line 14). He outlines the course of his day through the shifts in time in the passage which move gradually from his optimistic early morning start (line 1) to the first night away (line 33). These shifts in time seem to coincide with shifts in his feelings and as the day progresses we see him having doubts and anxieties about his trip. This is reflected in the short, simple sentences, 'I was free', 'It's all yours', whose forms seem to make sharp reminders of the downside of leaving home, of the freedom he wanted and leave the reader also feeling his regret and anxiety.

accurate terminology and a whole range of examples so far

very clearly explained

a perceptive comment

more accurate identification and examples

another perceptive comment

All Level 3 with some perceptive comments: 7 marks

Planning and writing a description from a picture stimulus

You are learning to:
- apply your knowledge of structure to your own creative writing
- use paragraphing and topic sentences effectively
- improve the range of vocabulary and language features in your own creative writing
- write a plan for a well-structured piece of creative writing from a picture stimulus.

Testing: AO5 and AO6
For: Paper 1 Question 5

1 Getting you thinking

When writing with the purpose of **describing**, you are transforming a visual picture into a piece of writing. Your reader should be able to 'see' the picture in their mind's eye.

In your study for AO2, you have already become familiar with a number of key structural techniques and language special effects. For Question 5, if you are given a descriptive task, this is your chance to use them just like a professional writer.

When we write in prose, our most logical way of showing order is to use paragraphs. Paragraphs show a logical change in writing, rather like the different stages in a journey.

a Look at the statements below. Are they true or false?

- Paragraphs should have a single focus.
- Paragraphs can go in any order.
- Paragraphs are there to make the page look neater.
- Paragraphs should begin with an introductory sentence.
- Paragraphs should be no more than 10 lines long.
- Paragraphs change to show a different time, place, person or subject.

2 Explore the skills

Planning and structuring your description

a Imagine you are going to write a description of the scene in the photograph on the following page, or another one of your choice. Pay close attention to the order your eye takes in the details of the photograph.

b Make a list of the different details you feel should be in your description. Ensure your list reflects the order in which you recorded each detail in your mind.

Here is a list that a student has compiled into a grid. They have put the details in a **logical order**. Each detail is going to be **the single focus** of a different paragraph of their description. They have gone on to start to write a clear introductory sentence – known as **a topic sentence** – for each paragraph.

c Help the student to finish the grid by writing possible topic sentences for paragraphs 3 and 4.

Detail from the picture	Topic sentence
Para 1: The large red house with blue shutters	Mandula's house dominated the bay of the small Greek fishing village.
Para 2: The sweep of soft sand	Like a continuing blanket of comfort, the sweep of soft sand always dried swiftly in the sun at low tide.
Para 3: The blueness of the sea and the sky	
Para 4: The figure in blue	
Para 5: The boats on the shore	Dotted along the shore, the tiny boats with their bright paint were a reminder of the struggling livelihood of the locals.

d By placing the details here in **a logical order** from the most obvious to the more subtle, how do you think this will add interest to the description?

e Does each paragraph deal with **one place**, **person** or **subject**? How will this allow the writer to develop more depth to their ideas?

③ Develop the skills

a Take a look at this extract from the writing mark scheme, which shows the lower Level 3 skills.

Lower Level 3 13–15 marks	**Content** • Register is generally matched to audience • Generally matched to purpose • Vocabulary clearly chosen for effect and appropriate use of linguistic features **Organisation** • Usually effective use of structural features • Writing is engaging with a range of connected ideas • Usually coherent paragraphs

The examiner is expecting you to:

- organise your work logically into paragraphs
- use some interesting structural special effects
- use interesting vocabulary and some language special effects
- stick to describing – don't slip into informing, narrating or persuading your reader into something
- keep your work appropriate for the reader.

Choosing language for your description

b Look at the flashcards below. For each flashcard, write your own definition.

Then write an example of each feature that you could use to describe an aspect of the picture. For example:

> Simile: a comparison using 'like' or 'as'
>
> The soft sand was like a continuing blanket of comfort.

Exam tip

In the examination, imagine the examiner cannot see the picture you have been given to write about. Bring it to life for your reader, so they can see in their mind's eye exactly what you see in the picture (and perhaps more besides!).

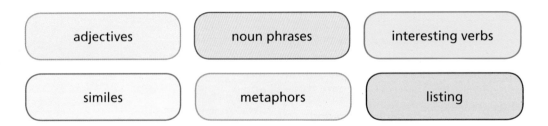

adjectives	noun phrases	interesting verbs
similes	metaphors	listing

c Below is an example of a student writing the opening paragraph to this description. How many different descriptive language features can you find in the paragraph?

Mandula's house dominated the bay of the small Greek fishing village. Painted in a deep ruby red, it made a striking sight against the deep blues of the Corfu sky. Its shutters were a contrast, a pretty turquoise, which mirrored the clear waters which lapped on the beach just a stone's throw away. The house stood proud and tall, with a kind face, like a watchful old fisherman watching the comings and goings of the tiny boats on the shore.

d Using this paragraph as your style model, go on to write paragraph 2 of the description based on the plan from **Explore the skills**.

4 Final task

- Look carefully at this very different picture of a lighthouse.

> **Think back**
> to the work you did in Week 7 where you thought about the effects of changing adjectives to modify the picture they create in your mind's eye.

- Write a structured five-point paragraph plan with topic sentences using the method from **Explore the skills**.
- Plan a selection of interesting language and structural special effects to include in the description.
- Go on to write up the first two paragraphs of your plan in approximately 15 minutes.

Planning and writing a description from a written stimulus

You are learning to:
- plan for a well-structured, well-organised response in the examination
- explore a method of planning through self-questioning
- construct a detailed plan for a description
- improve the range of vocabulary and language features in your own creative writing.

Testing: AO5 and AO6
For: Paper 1 Question 5

1 Getting you thinking

Think for one minute about your journey into class today.

Chances are that most days this involves a clear routine, a set route of places that you are likely to be by a certain time. The bus stop perhaps, the newsagents to pick up a snack, a specific spot to meet a friend. Your journey has a structure and a sequence that allows you to get where you want to be, logically and without confusion.

a Picture your journey into class in five clear stages.

b Can you remember a time when you were in a strange place – perhaps on holiday? What does it feel like to try and set out to find somewhere in a strange place?

A piece of writing without a clear structure makes the reader feel as perhaps you did in your strange place. That is why, in descriptive writing as well as in a narrative, structure is important.

In the examination, if you are asked to write a description, you may be given a topic. Your examination task would then look like the example below.

Write a description of a busy railway station.

You will have 45 minutes to complete your writing task, so in that limited time to show all of your best skills, you need to be very organised.

It may seem worrying to have to plan your work first, but this will stop you running into difficulties in your writing. Always aim to spend:

- 10–15 minutes planning your work
- 25–30 minutes writing your piece
- 5 minutes checking – there will be mistakes.

② Explore the skills

Look at the examination task. It may seem daunting as to how to begin. However, by learning how to **ask questions** yourself, you will have a much better chance of answering the exam questions well.

To plan for a topic-based description, aim to visualise the place, person or thing in your mind's eye. You are now going to undertake a **planning journey**.

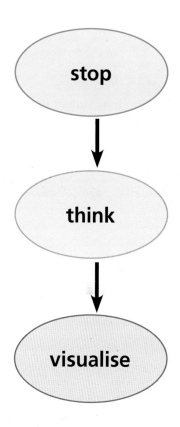

a Close your eyes and imagine you are about to step into a busy station.

- Read the prompts on Signpost 1 of the diagram on the following page.
- Spend one minute **exactly** jotting down everything you see in your mind's eye.
- Now repeat this for each of the other signposts.

1 As you walk into the busy station, what do you see?

- Think about the number of people around you.
- How are they moving?

Pinpoint one detail about the people. Now write down what you see.

2 Zoom in on one individual or couple – what do you see?

- An elderly man struggling with a suitcase?
- A young mum with a buggy?

Pinpoint one detail about the people. Now write down what you see.

3 As well as being surrounded by people you are surrounded by noise. What do you hear?

- The announcer over the intercom?
- Footsteps?
- People on mobile phones?

Now write down what you hear.

4 You look towards the ticket machines. What do you see?

- Impatient queues?
- A hassled woman who has dropped her purse?
- A young man who has lost his bank card?

Write down what you see.

5 You move towards the café. Look at the sandwiches and cakes on display. Who is in here?

- Morning commuters in a rush?
- Tourists with oversized bags?
- Look at the faces of the servers behind the counter – how is their day going?

Write down what you see.

6 You move now towards the platform for the train.

- How many platforms are there?
- How many trains are in?
- Where are they heading?
- What's the sound of their engines?
- How quick is the turnaround of passengers arriving and passengers leaving?
- Can you still hear the voice of the announcer?

Write down what you see and hear.

In no more than 10 minutes you have created a plan that will allow you to:

- write five well-organised paragraphs
- include a whole range of ideas, linked well
- have a logical structure or sequence in your description.

> **Think back**
>
> to Week 11, Lesson 1 and develop a **topic sentence** for each of your five planned paragraphs.

③ Develop the skills

a Look at these ideas collected by a student in response to Signpost 1.

It's packed – hundreds of people, all heading towards me it seems, suitcases on wheels, people dodging around each other

others ambling along texting, getting in everyone's way

business types in suits pouring off the London train – briefcases, raincoats

There is an elderly lady – two large zipped bags – on her own, hobbling slowly, scarf on her head, she looks fragile and vulnerable.

Think back
Using the flashcards from Week 11, Lesson 1, write up this student's opening paragraph and bring this description to life by including at least three features such as:

- adjectives
- noun phrases
- interesting verbs
- similes
- metaphors
- listing.

b Go on to write up a second paragraph of your own choice, from your own plan, including descriptive features.

c Now look at this response by a student and the notes from the examiner.

The station is chocka with people all scurrying like ants to their trains or to work or to meet their loved ones. There are bags and suitcases littering the ground and no one seems to have a minute to stop. Through the crowd there is an old man, in a long overcoat, with a trilby hat on his head. He carries an old battered suitcase that has seen better days. It looks like he is walking in slow motion through the fast-moving crowds.

The announcer is calling out platforms and places over the intercom but no one can hear what she is saying over the noise of the crowds and their constant footsteps. Music blares from people's earphones. Mobile phones are ringing. People are constantly chattering and shouting at their children to not run off.

Railway workers in uniform look like they are very bored clipping the tickets of the harassed passengers as they enter the platforms. The trains are lined up like soldiers in their smart red and blue colours. The express trains look ultra modern as they get ready to dash from city to city but the local trains look shabby as though no one cares about them.

Over the sounds of the loud speaker and the crowds shrill whistles blow and the trains chug tiredly out of the station carrying their heavy loads.

Examiner comment:

This answer describes all the way through and does not slip into telling a story. It has paragraphs which have linked ideas. The present tense is used all the way through. There is some attempt to use interesting vocabulary but this could be developed and occasional linguistic devices, though again, these could be improved. I would place this response in Lower Level 3 for AO5.

4 Final task

a Thinking about the examiner's comment on the above response, go on to write up the remaining three paragraphs from your own plan, including a range of descriptive features, in no more than 20 minutes.

Checklist for success

- Use your structured five-point planning journey.
- Remember to use topic sentences to make the focus of each paragraph clear.
- Plan a selection of interesting language and structural special effects to include in the description.

b Using the mark scheme in Week 8, Lesson 1, evaluate whether your response is:

- stronger than
- weaker than
- similar to

the example response in **Develop the skills**.

Introducing critical evaluation

You are learning to:
- understand what is meant by the term 'critical evaluation'
- see how this question brings together all of your reading skills
- ask yourself useful questions about unseen texts to explore both AO1 and AO2 in a text
- use a fiction text to practise reading for meaning (AO1)
- use a fiction text to practise analysing language and structure (AO2).

Testing: AO4
For: Paper 1 Question 4

1 Getting you thinking

At the end of your reading section on Paper 1, you will have a longer 20-mark answer to complete. This will be a 'mini essay', bringing together all of the skills in reading you have worked on so far.

This skill is called **critical evaluation**. 'Critical' reading does not mean being negative or picking faults. Instead, it means you examine and respond to the text in detail, working like a detective on the following:

- **AO1 skills:** making supported statements with inferences and your

- **AO2 skills:** analysing language and structure and its effects to make

- **AO4:** evaluating texts critically and supporting this with appropriate textual references.

'Evaluating' means weighing up all of those ideas and evidence to piece together what *you* think is the key meaning of the text you are working on – your *interpretation*. In your task, you will be asked to form an interpretation of your own.

You might think of it as:

$$AO1 + AO2 = AO4$$

For this task, again working with an unseen source, it is important to develop the skill of being able to **ask questions** about the text in order to plan effectively. In this way, it is useful to have some **thinking prompts** to help you to do this.

> **Think back**
>
> You can remind yourself of your AO1 and AO2 skills by revisiting Week 1, Lesson 1.

a Look at the **thinking prompts** below. Which of these prompts are AO1 skills and which of them are AO2 skills?

> What statements could I make based on the focus of the task? What are the key words?

> What kind of language/structural special effects has the writer used?

> Which parts of the text support my statements?

> What inferences can I draw from my quotations?

> What effects are created by the language/structure choices made by the writer?

② Explore the skills

a Read the extract on the following page, which is from *The Kite Runner* by Khaled Hosseini. Amir is a 12-year-old boy whose best friend, Hassan, is the son of his father's servant. Through reading to Hassan, Amir makes a discovery about himself. The story is set in Afghanistan.

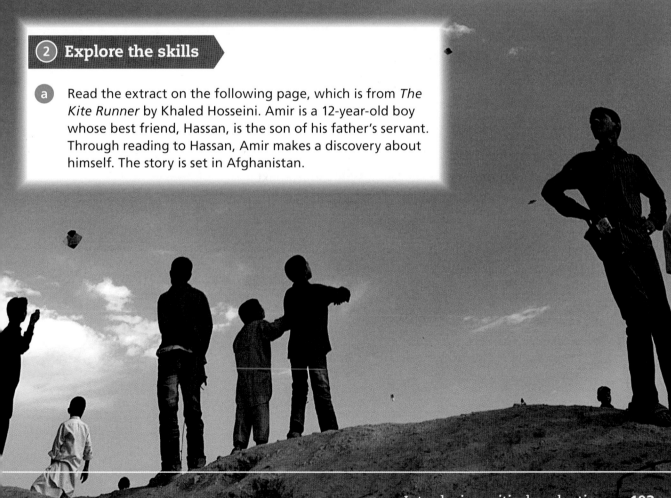

As you read, think about the following questions:

- What is this extract about?
- What are we learning about?
- How has the writer used language, narrative technique and an interesting structure to communicate ideas to the reader?

Sitting cross-legged, sunlight and shadows of pomegranate leaves dancing on his face, Hassan absently plucked blades of grass from the ground as I read him stories he couldn't read for himself. That Hassan would grow up illiterate [...] had been decided the minute he had been born, perhaps even the moment he had been conceived [...] – after all, what use did a servant have for the written word? But despite his illiteracy, or maybe because of it, Hassan was drawn to the mystery of words, seduced by a secret world forbidden to him. I read him poems and stories, sometimes riddles – though I stopped reading him those when I saw he was far better at solving them than I was. [...]

One day I played a little trick on Hassan. I was reading to him, and suddenly I strayed from the written story. I pretended I was reading from the book, flipping pages regularly, but I had abandoned the text altogether, taken over the story, and made up my own. Hassan, of course, was oblivious to this. To him, the words on the page were a scramble of codes, indecipherable, mysterious. Words were secret doorways and I held all the keys. After, I started to ask him if he liked the story, a giggle rising in my throat, when Hassan began to clap.

'What are you doing?' I said.

'That was the best story you've read me in a long time,' he said, still clapping.

I laughed. 'Really?'

'Really.'

'That's fascinating.' I muttered. I meant it too. This was…wholly unexpected. 'Are you sure, Hassan?'

He was still clapping. 'It was great, Amir. Will you read me more of it tomorrow?' [...]

I gave him a friendly shove. Smiled. 'You're a prince, Hassan. You're a prince and I love you.'

Khaled Hosseini, from *The Kite Runner*

b Write down your responses to these three colour-coded AO1 questions.

Remember that for AO1 you use the method:

Statement + Quotation + Inference

- What do we learn about Hassan?
- What do we learn about Amir and how he treats Hassan?
- What does Amir discover about himself through his friendship with Hassan?

③ Develop the skills

Now you are going to gather some evidence about the language and structure used by the writer in this extract.

a Make some notes on the effect and impact of the following words, phrases and structures using your AO2 skills.

Remember that for AO2 you use the method:

Feature + Example + Effect

Remember that for 'effect' you comment on what the feature makes you:

Think about   Feel   Imagine

- 'illiterate'   'the mystery of words'   'a secret world' 'what use did a servant have for the written word?'

- 'a little trick'   'pretended'   'a scramble of codes, indecipherable, mysterious'   'Words were secret doorways and I held all the keys'

- dialogue   questions   'clapping'   'friendly shove'   'Smiled'   'a prince'

④ Final task

You are now going to gather all of your ideas and notes together into a clear planning grid to answer the following examination task. You will move on to put together your response in Week 12, Lesson 2.

> **This extract tells us a lot about the nature of the friendship and relationship of the two boys. To what extent do you agree?**
>
> In your response you could:
>
> - consider your own impressions of the boys' friendship and relationship
>
> - evaluate how the writer presents the friendship and relationship
>
> - support your opinions with quotations from the text.

Exam tip

By working in this way, you will have planned enough material to enable you to create a successful mini essay for Paper 1 Question 4 and cover all of the bullet points in the mark scheme.

a Copy and complete the planning grid below with all of your ideas.

	What do we learn?	Supporting quotation	Inference	What does the writer use?	Example	Effect
Idea for a)						
Idea for b)						
Idea for c)						

Developing critical evaluation skills

You are learning to:
- understand the critical evaluation examination task
- explore a student response and think about the mark scheme skills
- practise writing part of a response yourself
- consider opening and ending your response
- write a complete response.

Testing: AO4
For: Paper 1 Question 4

1 Getting you thinking

a Look closely at the examination task you planned in Week 12, Lesson 1 and the notes in the annotations.

In Question 4 you will always be given a statement to base your interpretation on. You can agree or disagree with the statement but you have to support your ideas well.

This extract tells us a lot about the nature of the friendship and relationship of the two boys. To what extent do you agree?

In your response you could:

- consider your own impressions of the boys' friendship and relationship
- evaluate how the writer presents the friendship and relationship
- support your opinions with quotations from the text.

(20 marks)

This says 'could' but it is a useful guide to all of the skills you need to show.

This is asking **what** you learn about the boy's friendship and so is an AO1 skill.

This is asking **how** the writer presents their ideas and is an AO2 skill.

This reminds you to support all of your ideas with the text. It is useful to remember to give examples of language and structure.

This question is worth as much as Q1 + Q2 + Q3 all together. You must keep **half** of your planning and writing time on the reading section for this task.

2 Explore the skills

a Look at this opening to a response to the examination task, piecing together the thinking prompts you have been working on.

We learn in the extract that Hassan and Amir are friends but Amir is the only one who can read. In contrast, 'Hassan would grow up illiterate', which suggests there is a difference in the status of the two boys. The writer emphasises the difference in their status through the use of the question, 'what use did a servant have…written word?', which makes me feel that Amir did not question whether or not this was fair or right.

We also learn that Hassan is very interested in reading and stories and riddles, 'far better at solving them than I was'. This implies that Hassan is very bright and would be an able boy if he had the chance. The writer shows this by using the metaphor of 'a secret world' and words such as 'mystery', 'secret' and 'forbidden' which makes me think of how unfair and unequal the relationship between the boys is.

b In the answer can you identify:

- some clear statements linked to the focus of the task?
- quotations to support those statements?
- inferences to show understanding?
- where language and structural features have been pointed out?
- where there are examples of these?
- whether there are any comments on effect and are they clear to you?

c Now look at this extract from the mark scheme for Question 4.

Level 4 Perceptive, detailed **16–20 marks**	Shows perceptive and detailed evaluation: • Critically and in detail evaluates the effects • Shows perceptive understanding of writer's methods • Selects a judicious range of textual references • Develops a convincing and perceptive response to the focus of the task
Level 3 Clear, relevant **11–15 marks**	Shows clear and relevant evaluation: • Clearly evaluates the effects • Shows clear understanding of writer's methods • Selects a range of relevant textual references • Makes a clear and relevant response to the focus of the task
Level 2 Some, attempts **6–10 marks**	Shows some attempts at evaluation: • Makes some evaluative comment(s) on effect • Shows some understanding of writer's methods • Selects some appropriate textual references • Makes some response to the focus of the task

- Identify the ladder of skills and match those skills against the thinking prompts you learned in Week 12, Lesson 1.
- Thinking about the skills you identified in the answer, what mark would you give the student response above and why?

③ **Develop the skills**

a Using the student response as your style guide for success, go on to write up the next section of this response using your completed planning grid from Week 12, Lesson 1. Remember to link together your AO1 and AO2 ideas to make the blend of skills for AO4.

b Now look at these opening and concluding sentences.

> This extract tells us a lot about the nature of the friendship and relationship of the two boys.
>
> I agree with the statement.
>
> This extract presents Amir and Hassan's relationship in a complex way. In the first instance we learn that...
>
> Overall it is clear that the extract tells us a lot about the nature of the friendship and relationship of the two boys.
>
> To conclude, we see a strong message here about how the boys' friendship was strong, but how it also showed the injustice and inequality of their relationship.
>
> So, yes, I do agree with the statement.

Exam tip

Always bear in mind the key words from the mark scheme descriptors:

Level 1: Simple, limited
Level 2: Some, attempts
Level 3: Clear, relevant
Level 4: Detailed, perceptive

Where would you like to be?

- Which of these sentences would make an answer feel simple and **limited**?
- Which of these sentences shows an **attempt** to evaluate?
- Which of the sentences opens up the possibilities for some **clear**, or even **perceptive** evaluation?

④ Final task

Using:

- your planning grid from Week 12, Lesson 1
- your style guide from **Explore the skills**
- your own work from **Develop the skills (a)**
- the clearest sentence openers from **Develop the skills (b)**

write a complete response to the examination task in not more that 20–25 minutes.

> **This extract tells us a lot about the nature of the friendship and relationship of the two boys. To what extent do you agree?**
>
> In your response you could:
>
> - consider your own impressions of the boys' friendship and relationship
> - evaluate how the writer presents the friendship and relationship
> - support your opinions with quotations from the text.
>
> **(20 marks)**

Applying critical evaluation skills to Paper 1 Question 4

You are learning to:
- practise an examination task, step by step
- include your AO1 comprehension skills in your response (lower order skills)
- include your AO2 language and structural analysis skills in your response (higher order skills)
- explore a student response
- write your own complete response.

Testing: AO4
For: Paper 1 Question 4

① Getting you thinking

You are now going to work through a Question 4 task. The following extract is from a short story, 'The Veldt', by Ray Bradbury, about a family who live in a technology-filled house with gadgets that do everything for them. The children's room is a virtual reality room that is able to connect with the children telepathically to reproduce any place they imagine.

 a As you read, think about the following examination task:

> **'The Veldt' is a story that seems to warn us about the use of too much technology in our lives. To what extent do you agree?**
>
> In your response, you could:
>
> - consider your own impressions of the technology in the children's room
> - evaluate how the writer presents the disturbing atmosphere
> - support your opinions with quotations from the text.

They walked down the hall of their soundproofed Happylife Home, which had cost them thirty thousand dollars installed, this house which clothed and fed and rocked them to sleep and played and sang and was good to them.

Their approach sensitized a switch somewhere and the nursery light flicked on when they came within ten feet of it. [...]

'Well,' said George Hadley.

They stood on the thatched floor of the nursery. It was forty feet across by forty feet long and thirty feet high; it had cost half again as much as the rest of the house. 'But nothing's too good for our children,' George had said.

The nursery was silent. It was empty as a jungle glade at hot high noon. The walls were blank and two dimensional. Now, as George and Lydia Hadley stood in the center of the room, the walls began to purr and recede into crystalline distance, it seemed, and presently an African veldt appeared, in three dimensions, on all sides, in color reproduced to the final pebble and bit of straw. The ceiling above them became a deep sky with a hot yellow sun.

George Hadley felt the perspiration start on his brow.

'Let's get out of this sun,' he said. 'This is a little too real. But I don't see anything wrong.'

'Wait a moment, you'll see,' said his wife.

Now the hidden odorophonics were beginning to blow a wind of odor at the two people. The hot straw smell of lion grass, [...] the great rusty smell of animals, the smell of dust like a red paprika in the hot air. And now the sounds: the thump of distant antelope feet on grassy sod, the papery rustling of vultures. [...]

'You see, there are the lions, far over, that way. Now they're on their way to the water hole. They've just been eating,' said Lydia. 'I don't know what.'

'Some animal.' George Hadley put his hand up to shield off the burning light from his squinted eyes. 'A zebra or a baby giraffe, maybe.'

'Are you sure?' His wife sounded peculiarly tense.

'No, it's a little late to be sure,' he said, amused. 'Nothing over there I can see but cleaned bone, and the vultures dropping for what's left.'

'Did you hear that scream?' she asked.

'No.'

'About a minute ago?'

'Sorry, no.'

The lions were coming. And again George Hadley was filled with admiration for the mechanical genius who had conceived this room.

[...] Every home should have one. Oh, occasionally they frightened you with their clinical accuracy, they startled you, gave you a twinge, but most of the time what fun for everyone, not only your own son and daughter, but for yourself when you felt like a quick jaunt to a foreign land, a quick change of scenery. Well, here it was!

And here were the lions now, fifteen feet away, so real, so feverishly and startlingly real that you could feel the prickling fur on your hand, and your mouth was stuffed with the dusty upholstery smell of their heated pelts, and the yellow of them was in your eyes like the yellow of an exquisite French tapestry, the yellows of lions and summer grass, and the sound of the matted lion lungs exhaling on the silent noontide, and the smell of meat from the panting, dripping mouths.

The lions stood looking at George and Lydia Hadley with terrible green-yellow eyes.

'Watch out!' screamed Lydia.

The lions came running at them.

Ray Bradbury, from 'The Veldt'

② Explore the skills

a Now think about gathering your ideas for the first bullet point of the task.

- consider your own impressions of the technology in the children's room

Think about:

- What do I learn about the technology in the children's room?

Think about the cost and the extent of it. Does it sound amazing or unpleasant?

- What do I learn about the parents' different feelings about it?

What does the father feel about it? How about the mother? Why is she concerned? Where are the children?

- What do I learn about the impact of the virtual reality on the parents?

How realistic does the experience become? What seems to be happening?

b Now write three clear **statements**.

Support each statement with a **quotation** from the text.

Make an **inference** for each one.

Level 3	Shows clear and relevant evaluation:	
Clear, relevant	• Clearly evaluates the effects	Higher order skills
11–15 marks	• Shows clear understanding of writer's methods	
	• Selects a range of relevant textual references	Lower order skills
	• Makes a clear and relevant response to the focus of the task	

③ Develop the skills

You are now going to tackle the higher order skills of the mark scheme and gather ideas for the second bullet point of the task:

- evaluate how the writer presents the disturbing atmosphere.

a From each colour-coded section of text, gather at least *one* language or structural feature. Make a note of it and add your example, reference or quotation.

b Read this student response and the examiner comments.

Technology seems to have a very positive impact in the story at first as it tells us 'this house which clothed and fed and rocked them to sleep and played and sang and was good to them'. It seems like the technology does everything and makes life a lot easier.

— presents a useful idea and uses a key word from the question. The quotation is a little lengthy. Makes an inference

But the story goes on to say it is also negative. George says at one point, 'This is a little too real', implying things are getting a bit much especially in the nursery where the technology makes it seem like Africa.

— sees another possibility and makes an inference, though not developed

This scene is so real it seems to be very scary, especially for children. The mum is very scared of the lions even though they are not real but they are very frightening. 'The lions stood looking at George and Lydia Hadley with terrible green-yellow eyes'. I agree this is warning us about the dangers of technology as it makes me think of how we are warned about video games and the dangers of the internet today. How it can be risky.

— links the point usefully to the question

The parents also seem to have different attitudes which is also like people today. The mum is frightened and warning her husband about what they have let the children play with but he is not listening to the warning saying, 'crystal walls, that's all they are'. He is not thinking about the impact on his children.

— is thinking carefully about the message of the text or the 'warning' and presents a strong idea here

- Which skills from the mark scheme has this candidate included?
- Which skills have they missed out?
- What level of the mark scheme do you think this candidate is working at and why?

④ Final task

Write up your own improved response to the task in no more than 20–25 minutes.

Checklist for success

- Use all of your AO1 + AO2 planning.
- Aim to improve on the student response in **Develop the skills (b)**.
- Remember to include an opening evaluative statement and a closing evaluative statement linked to the focus of the task.

End-of-term progress assessment task: Walking through a mock Paper 1

You are aiming to show that:
- you can read an unseen fiction text carefully and with understanding, picking out the right types of information
- you have some knowledge about the language and language features used in the text and the effect those choices have on you the reader
- you have some knowledge about how that fiction text can be structured and the effect this has on you, the reader.

Testing: AO1 and AO2
For: Paper 1 Questions 1, 2 and 3

What you can expect in the exam

In Paper 1 Section A of the exam, you will be asked to read a piece of source material form a short story or novel from the 20th or 21st century. You are unlikely to have seen the passage before.

Your job is to apply your skills of reading and analysis to answer the questions about the passage.

You have **one hour** to read and complete **four** questions worth **40 marks** – half of the marks for the paper.

Step 1

Begin by reading the extract below carefully.

> There was music from my neighbour's house through the summer nights. In his blue gardens men and girls came and went like moths among the whisperings and the champagne and the stars. At high tide in the afternoon I watched his guests diving from the tower of his raft, or taking the sun on the hot sand of his beach while his two motor-boats
> 5 slit the waters of the Sound, drawing aquaplanes over cataracts of foam. On week-ends his Rolls-Royce became an omnibus, bearing parties to and from the city between nine in the morning and long past midnight, while his station wagon scampered like a brisk yellow bug to meet all trains. And on Mondays eight servants, including an extra gardener, toiled all day with mops and scrubbing-brushes and hammers and garden-shears, repairing the
> 10 ravages of the night before.
>
> Every Friday five crates of oranges and lemons arrived from a fruiterer in New York — every Monday these same oranges and lemons left his back door in a pyramid of pulpless halves. There was a machine in the kitchen which could extract the juice of two hundred oranges in half an hour if a little button was pressed two hundred times by a butler's thumb.

15 At least once a fortnight a corps of caterers came down with several hundred feet of canvas
and enough colored lights to make a Christmas tree of Gatsby's enormous garden. On buffet
tables, garnished with glistening hors-d'oeuvre, spiced baked hams crowded against salads
of harlequin designs and pastry pigs and turkeys bewitched to a dark gold. In the main hall
a bar with a real brass rail was set up, and stocked with gins and liquors and with cordials
20 so long forgotten that most of his female guests were too young to know one from another.

By seven o'clock the orchestra has arrived, no thin five-piece affair, but a whole pitful of
oboes and trombones and saxophones and viols and cornets and piccolos, and low and
high drums. The last swimmers have come in from the beach now and are dressing up-
stairs; the cars from New York are parked five deep in the drive, and already the halls and
25 salons and verandas are gaudy with primary colors, and hair bobbed in strange new ways,
and shawls beyond the dreams of Castile. The bar is in full swing, and floating rounds of
cocktails permeate the garden outside, until the air is alive with chatter and laughter, and
casual innuendo and introductions forgotten on the spot, and enthusiastic meetings between
women who never knew each other's names.

30 The lights grow brighter as the earth lurches away from the sun, and now the orchestra
is playing yellow cocktail music, and the opera of voices pitches a key higher. Laughter
is easier minute by minute, spilled with prodigality, tipped out at a cheerful word. The
groups change more swiftly, swell with new arrivals, dissolve and form in the same breath;
already there are wanderers, confident girls who weave here and there among the stouter
35 and more stable, become for a sharp, joyous moment the centre of a group, and then, excited
with triumph, glide on through the sea-change of faces and voices and colour under the
constantly changing light.

F. Scott Fitzgerald, from *The Great Gatsby*

Step 2

Now read the first examination task and write out your answer carefully. This is testing your basic skills for AO1.

> 1. **Read again the first part of the source highlighted in blue. List four things you learn from the extract about the narrator's neighbour.**
>
> **(4 marks)**

Checklist for success

- Present your response to Question 1 in a numbered list.
- Use short, sharp clear sentences.
- Use only things that are given to you in the extract and that you can identify as being true.

Step 3

When you are happy with your response, move on to the next task. This is testing your skills for AO2.

> 2. **Look in detail at the section highlighted in yellow.**
>
> **How does the writer use language here to describe the neighbour's (Gatsby's) party?**
>
> You could include the writer's choice of:
>
> - words and phrases
> - language features and techniques
> - sentence forms.
>
> **(8 marks)**

Checklist for success

- Select no more than three language ideas or special effects.
- Make sure you give an example of each one.
- Make a comment that explains its effect by deciding on what it makes you think of, feel or imagine.

Step 4

When you are happy with your response, move on to the next task. This is also testing your skills for AO2.

3. **You now need to think about the whole of the source.**

   This text is an extract from a novel.

   How has the writer structured the text to interest you, as a reader?

   You could write about:

   - what the writer focuses your attention on at the beginning
   - how and why the writer changes the focus as the source develops
   - any other structural features that interest you. **(8 marks)**

Checklist for success

- Select no more than three structural ideas or special effects.
- Give an example of each one or indicate where they are with a line reference.
- Make a comment that explains what the feature does to the text and the effect this has on you, the reader.

End-of-term progress assessment task: Walking through a mock Paper 1

You are aiming to show that:
- you have a more developed understanding of the unseen fiction text by being able to back up your thoughts with evidence
- you can make suggestions about what the text might mean or suggest to you
- you have some knowledge about the language and language features used in the text and the effect those choices have on you, the reader
- you have some knowledge about how a fiction text can be structured and the effect this has on you, the reader.

Testing: AO4
For: Paper 1 Question 4

In this second End-of-term progress assessment task, you are going to complete the final question (Question 4) of Section A.

This question tests AO4.

It represents 20 of the 40 marks for Section A.

You will find it helpful to read the whole extract from last time before you begin.

Question 4 will ask you to focus on a larger section of the source material – approximately half of the extract.

Step 1

Carefully read the selected extract from *The Great Gatsby*.

> At least once a fortnight a corps of caterers came down with several hundred feet of canvas and enough colored lights to make a Christmas tree of Gatsby's enormous garden. On buffet tables, garnished with glistening hors-d'oeuvre, spiced baked hams crowded against salads of harlequin designs and pastry pigs
> 5 and turkeys bewitched to a dark gold. In the main hall a bar with a real brass rail was set up, and stocked with gins and liquors and with cordials so long forgotten that most of his female guests were too young to know one from another.

By seven o'clock the orchestra has arrived, no thin five-piece affair, but a whole
pitful of oboes and trombones and saxophones and viols and cornets and
10 piccolos, and low and high drums. The last swimmers have come in from the
beach now and are dressing up-stairs; the cars from New York are parked five
deep in the drive, and already the halls and salons and verandas are gaudy
with primary colors, and hair bobbed in strange new ways, and shawls beyond
the dreams of Castile. The bar is in full swing, and floating rounds of cocktails
15 permeate the garden outside, until the air is alive with chatter and laughter,
and casual innuendo and introductions forgotten on the spot, and enthusiastic
meetings between women who never knew each other's names.

The lights grow brighter as the earth lurches away from the sun, and now the
orchestra is playing yellow cocktail music, and the opera of voices pitches a key
20 higher. Laughter is easier minute by minute, spilled with prodigality, tipped out
at a cheerful word. The groups change more swiftly, swell with new arrivals,
dissolve and form in the same breath; already there are wanderers, confident
girls who weave here and there among the stouter and more stable, become for a
sharp, joyous moment the centre of a group, and then, excited with triumph, glide
25 on through the sea-change of faces and voices and colour under the constantly
changing light.

F. Scott Fitzgerald, from *The Great Gatsby*

Step 2

Now read your examination task for Question 4 and plan your
answer carefully before writing it out. This is testing your skills
for AO4.

Question 4

Focus your answer on this second part of the source.

**A student, having read this section of the text, said: 'F. Scott
Fitzgerald creates a real sense of wealth and glamour in his
description.'**

To what extent do you agree?

In your response, you could:

- consider your own impressions of Gatsby's party
- evaluate how the writer creates a sense of wealth and
  glamour
- support your opinions with quotations from the text.

(20 marks)

End-of-term progress assessment task: Walking through a mock Paper 1

You are aiming to show that:
- you can select and plan an examination task testing either descriptive or narrative writing
- you can use paragraphing and topic sentences effectively
- you can apply your knowledge of structure and use interesting structural features in your own creative writing
- you can apply your knowledge of language and use a range of vocabulary and language features in your own creative writing
- you can include some accurate complex spellings
- you can control the tense of your verbs and agreement
- you can punctuate your work in a way that shows you are clear and accurate
- you can vary your sentences for effect.

Testing: AO5 and AO6
For: Paper 1 Question 5

In this final session of your Paper 1 mock exam, you are going to complete Section B of the paper, testing AO5 and AO6 and representing 40 marks.

You are advised to spend 45 minutes on the exam task. You must write in full sentences.

You are reminded of the need to plan your answer.

You should leave enough time to check your work at the end.

Step 1

Select and complete one of the tasks below.

Question 5

Either:

Write a description suggested by this picture:

Or:

Write a short story about a time when a party or celebration went badly wrong.

Checklist for success

- Write a structured five-point planning journey.
- Remember to use topic sentences.
- Plan a selection of interesting language and structural special effects to include in the description.

Checklist for success

- Ensure your story has an effective opening, a complication, a climax and resolution.
- Ensure you have paragraphed each of these shifts clearly.

Step 2

Check back through your spelling and punctuation to ensure it makes your work clear, effective and varied.

(24 marks for content and organisation
16 marks for technical accuracy)   **(40 marks)**

Check your progress: Section A

Grade 8

- I can summarise and critically evaluate with detailed and perceptive understanding.
- I can understand and respond with insight to explicit and implicit meanings and viewpoints.
- I can analyse and critically evaluate detailed aspects of language, grammar and structure.
- I can back up my understanding and opinions with judicious references and supporting quotations.

Grade 5

- I can summarise and evaluate with accuracy and clear understanding.
- I can understand and make valid responses to explicit and implicit meanings and viewpoints.
- I can analyse and evaluate relevant aspects of language, grammar and structure.
- I can support my understanding and opinions with sensibly chosen references to texts.

Grade 2

- I can describe and summarise with some accuracy and understanding.
- I can respond in a straightforward way to most explicit information and viewpoints.
- I can make some relevant comments about language and structure.
- I can support my comments and opinions with some general references.

Check your progress: Section B

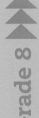

Grade 8

- I can communicate with impact.
- I can produce an ambitious and effectively structured piece of writing.
- I can use a wide range of well-selected sentence types and structures, and use precise vocabulary for impact.
- I can spell, punctuate and use grammar accurately so that writing is virtually error-free.

Grade 5

- I can communicate effectively and hold my reader's interest.
- I can produce a well-structured and purposeful piece of writing.
- I can vary my sentence types and structures, and use vocabulary for effect.
- I can spell, punctuate and use grammar accurately with occasional errors.

Grade 2

- I can communicate simply in English with some clarity for my reader.
- I can produce writing with a basic structure and some awareness of purpose.
- I can show some control over sentences and use familiar vocabulary.
- I can spell, punctuate and use grammar with a little accuracy.

Recapping basic comprehension skills

You are learning to:
- read non-fiction texts carefully and with understanding, picking out the right types of information
- make some deductions about what things might mean or suggest to you to show your understanding.

Testing: AO1
For: Paper 2 Question 1 (and building skills for Question 2)

① Getting you thinking

For Paper 2, you will be using all of the same skills you have learned for Paper 1, but this time, you will be applying them to **non-fiction** texts.

This time, for Question 1, rather than *listing* basic information from the text, you will need to do some detective work and form your own opinions as to what is **true** in the text and what is **false**.

a Carefully read this extract from a blog written by a man who had served a 25-year prison sentence.

Key term

non-fiction: a piece of writing, which is true, factual or about real-life events, for example, newspaper articles, blogs, biographies, autobiographies, letters, diaries, travel writing

HOME	ABOUT	SKILLS	CONTACT	BLOG

In order to prepare for my life upon release from prison, I used to wake very early. On the morning of Aug. 13, I remember waking before 3 am. I was confined inside of an open dormitory at the federal prison camp in Atwater. I sat at an empty table, amazed with the realization that my day had finally come. For decades I'd been waiting for my release date, but it always seemed so far away that I couldn't really grasp it. On that Monday morning, however, I woke with certainty that I was scheduled to walk out of prison gates.

A commitment to exercise carried me through the entire journey, and I did not waver on the morning that I was going to be released. I did my strength training inside with pushups, and I then walked outside to run. I finished my run at 6:15, then I returned to the housing unit for my shower and shave. Those activities felt different for me that morning because I still couldn't wrap my mind around the reality that in a few hours, authorities were going to release me. After dressing, I went outside to sit. I needed some alone time to gather my thoughts. I looked around at the track and wondered what it would feel like to walk out, and I also wondered how it was going to happen.

At 7:15, I heard an announcement over the institutional loudspeaker. It paged me to the rear gate of the prison. Many prisoners sent me good wishes as I walked over toward that gate, my bag in hand with the books that I was carrying out with me. A guard eventually stepped out to meet me at the gate, and he escorted me inside one of the penitentiary buildings. My legs felt rubbery for some reason, perhaps because I was walking in an area of the prison that had previously been forbidden to me. The administrative process took about 30 minutes, and that was it. The guard then escorted me through a series of gates and I saw my loving wife.

Michael Santos, from *Quora*, 25 January 2013

b Look at the following statements and, checking carefully with the extract, decide if each statement is **true** or **false**.

1. He had been waiting a few days for his release date.

2. The paperwork for his release took about half an hour.

3. The other prisoners were impolite to him as he left.

4. On the day of his release the prisoner woke up before 3 a.m.

5. On his release the prisoner was met outside by his daughter.

6. The prisoner did not believe in taking exercise.

7. He sat outside after getting dressed.

8. He was released on a Monday.

② Explore the skills

Just as earlier, when you investigated if a statement about the text was true or false, you will also need your skills in reading and understanding for Question 2 of the examination.

Think back

Remind yourself of these skills in Week 1, Lesson 2 and Week 2, Lesson 1.

a Read the opening of this piece of journalism from a broadsheet newspaper.

> No bell marks the start of our day. Instead, a slow drip-feed of men in grey tracksuits amble their way into classes. Sometimes 10 sit in front of me, aged 21 up to 60 or 70. They are the disaffected and the despicable. They are the proud, the defensive and the downright disagreeable; funnelled into education during their first days inside, where they complete assessments in literacy and numeracy. Their scores determine their placement into a classroom, and their subsequent opportunities for work.
>
> The Secret Teacher, from *The Guardian*, 3 May 2014

- Using your skills in making **inferences**, identify the place being described. Make a note of the clues that helped you decide.

- What do you understand about the people being described here?

- Would you say the writer has a positive or negative impression of the people he describes? Select two pieces of evidence for this.

Key term

inferences: the explanation of what you have been able to read between the lines

b Now read the second paragraph of the article.

The most challenging part of working with offenders is the disparity between students in the classroom – the range of ages, their level of literacy and their attitude to learning. Often their only common ground is their criminality. Some learners arrive spoiling for a fight, desperate to avoid the torture of school all over again, determined to prove themselves. Behaviour is an issue, with many refusing to work. Challenging inappropriate language is a constant battle when, for some, the f-word is used in every sentence.

The Secret Teacher, from *The Guardian*, 3 May 2014

- Does this paragraph add to or challenge your thoughts from the opening? What is your evidence?

- What viewpoint has been created of the prisoners so far?

③ Develop the skills

a Now read paragraph three of the article and think about the words and phrases that have been highlighted for you. Jot down what you can infer from each one.

> The biggest rewards working in offender learning come when someone makes you rethink your first impressions of them, when someone proves you wrong. A learner once came to my class, asked what subject it was, reeled off a load of expletives and refused to stay. He was a London lad, a football hooligan. Three weeks later, he returned, calmer, and took his seat. Three months later, I nominated him for an adult learner award because of his success in literacy. I saw him change from this thuggish brute with a bad attitude to one of the most dedicated learners I have had – he even went on to support a young man who was struggling. It's so satisfying as a tutor when, despite initial reluctance, your pupils relax, and begin to trust you and your teaching. They begin to realise that if they attend, and they listen, and they try, they can actually do this.

b Do you think the writer now has a positive or negative viewpoint about the prisoners?

c Has the writer made you think differently about the prisoners? Can you work out why?

d By this point, can you work out what job the writer of this article does?

④ **Final task**

You are now going to practise a Paper 2 Question 1 examination task. Re-read the extracts from Activities 2 and 3.

1. Choose four statements below that are TRUE.

    Choose a maximum of four statements. **(4 marks)**

    a) Teaching in a prison can be very satisfying for this tutor.

    b) When the prisoners first arrive they do tests in numeracy and literacy.

    c) Some of the prisoners use bad language.

    d) A young man from London was nominated for an adult learner award.

    e) The day begins with a school bell.

    f) The students are aged from 21 to 40.

    g) It is easy working with such a wide range of prisoners in the classroom.

    h) Behaviour is good in the prison classroom.

Developing comprehension skills with more than one text

You are learning to:
- read carefully and with understanding, picking out the right types of information
- show your understanding of what you read by being able to back up your thoughts with evidence
- make suggestions about what things might mean or suggest to you to show your understanding
- be able to do that with more than one text at once.

Testing: AO1
For: Paper 2 Question 2

① Getting you thinking

In Paper 2, you will be given two pieces of source material to work with, not one. Both pieces of source material will be non-fiction.

a Take a look at how Question 2 will be worded. Use the annotations to help you understand its format.

Paper 2 Question 2:

You need to refer to **Source A** and **Source B** for this question.

The expeditions of 1912 and 2008 had many things in common.

Use details from **both** sources to write a summary of the similarities.

(8 marks)

A reminder that you need to use both texts in your answer.

You will be given a statement about the two texts. It will present something that is similar about them or something that is different. Try to think: What do I learn about…the expeditions of 1912 and 2008 from the two texts?

You will then be asked to focus on **either** the similarities or the differences. But remember: this is still an AO1 basic comprehension task. A summary does not require a lot of detail. It means that when you present your ideas, you do so in a crisp, clear, concise way, making only the key points.

This is an 8-mark question, so not an essay. It is a short-answer response requiring no more than three key points.

② Explore the skills

a Look at these two short non-fiction extracts. Source A is from Captain Scott's diary recounting his doomed expedition to the South Pole in 1912. Source B is from *Race to the Pole*, an account of a race between six teams of explorers to conquer the South Pole in 2008.

Source A

We started at 7.30, none of us having slept much after the shock of our discovery. We followed the Norwegian sledge tracks for some way; as far as we make out there are only two men. In about three miles we passed two small cairns. Then the weather overcast, and the tracks being increasingly drifted up and obviously going too far to the west, we decided to make straight for the Pole according to our calculations. At 12.30 Evans had such cold hands we camped for lunch – an excellent 'week-end one'. [...] To-night little Bowers is laying himself out to get sights in terrible difficult circumstances; the wind is blowing hard, T. –21 degrees, and there is that curious damp, cold feeling in the air which chills one to the bone in no time.

From *Captain Scott's Diary*, 1912

Source B

The next day was one of those where the place you wake up in feels totally different from the one you went to bed in. Everything about the start of the next day was grey. The cloud cover and wind totally changed the appearance of the plateau; it was as if we'd been inside the tent for a month rather than a night, or as if we'd gone to bed in summer and woken up on the edges of winter. The sky was dark, the wind was already blowing hard and the temperature had dropped 15 degrees. With wind chill, it was down to minus 41.

James Cracknell and Ben Fogle, from *Race to the Pole*

In both extracts, we are given key information about:

- the place
- the weather
- the temperature.

b Collect together this information and remember to select quotations to use as evidence. Organise it in a chart or grid like the one below.

	In Source A I learn...	Evidence from the text	In Source B I learn...	Evidence from the text
The place				
The weather				
The temperature				

c Look at this example paragraph from a student, summarising the first key idea about the place and using their evidence concisely and usefully.

> Both sets of explorers are in a harsh, inhospitable place: for example, the tracks in Source A are described as 'drifted up' and it's impossible to see too far ahead, 'to get sights in terrible difficult circumstances.' In Source B, 'the sky was dark' and the environment has changed drastically overnight.
>
> The weather…

d Now complete a second paragraph, summarising your key ideas about the weather. Use your evidence to help you make your point.

③ Develop the skills

You are going to continue summarising the similarities between the expeditions of 1912 and 2008.

a Read these further extracts from both texts.

b What other key information categories are there? Add them to your notes or table.

c Add in your ideas and evidence.

Source A

After lunch, and Evans still not appearing, we looked out, to see him still afar off. By this time we were alarmed, and all four started back on ski. I was first to reach the poor man and shocked at his appearance; he was on his knees with clothing disarranged, hands uncovered and frostbitten, and a wild look in his eyes. Asked what was the matter, he replied with a slow speech that he didn't know, but thought he must have fainted. We got him on his feet, but after two or three steps he sank down again. He showed every sign of complete collapse. Wilson, Bowers, and I went back for the sledge, whilst Oates remained with him. When we returned he was practically unconscious, and when we got him into the tent quite comatose. He died quietly at 12.30 A.M.

It is a terrible thing to lose a companion in this way, but calm reflection shows that there could not have been a better ending to the terrible anxieties of the past week. Discussion of the situation at lunch yesterday shows us what a desperate pass we were in with a sick man on our hands at such a distance from home.

Source B

Ed came up alongside, then moved ahead and rammed his pole into the ground.

'We're stopping!' he stated defiantly. 'You're recovering from pneumonia, and you need to rest.'

'I'm OK; I can carry on,' I protested weakly.

'We're not carrying on. For the last three days we've done fewer kilometres each day, and for the last two days we've been all over the shop. We haven't even skied as a group. We need to rest, otherwise we'll be even weaker tomorrow.'

Suddenly all the anger and frustration came pouring out. 'I've let you down, my blisters have slowed us down, I've got pneumonia, frostbite and now I can't pull my weight. I trained so hard for this. I'm so sorry.'

④ **Final task**

You are now going to put together all of your ideas and evidence to complete the following examination task.

> **The expeditions of 1912 and 2008 had many things in common.**
>
> Use details from *both* sources to write a summary of the similarities.   **(8 marks)**

You could begin with the example paragraph from 2c and continue from there.

Checklist for success

- Ask yourself what the extracts have in common.
- Organise that information into logical categories.
- Select evidence that you can use in support.

Working with challenging vocabulary in 19th century texts

You are learning to:
- approach unseen 19th century texts for Paper 2 with more confidence
- explore some techniques for dealing with the vocabulary of unseen 19th century texts
- use your skills of inference to help you work out the meaning of unseen 19th century texts.

Testing: AO1, AO2, AO3
For: Paper 2 Section A

① Getting you thinking

On Paper 2, one of your sources will be relatively modern: from either the 20th or 21st century.

Your second source will be from the 19th century, so it may seem strange or unfamiliar and therefore challenging to read and understand.

Some of the main reasons why texts are challenging are that they:

- use unfamiliar vocabulary
- use unfamiliar or complex sentence structures
- refer to unfamiliar concepts or things that are outside your own experiences.

a Look at the extract below from an autobiography.

> In the latter part of my school life I became passionately fond of shooting

b What possible meanings might you be able to **infer** from this extract?

c What kind of person might have written this autobiography:

- a famous gangster
- someone with a deep interest in nature and wildlife
- an aristocrat with a country estate?

Key term

infer: conclude by reasoning what you have been able to read between the lines

② Explore the skills

Unfamiliar vocabulary can be unsettling, particularly in unseen texts. Instead of worrying about the unfamiliar, try to focus on the **familiar**, where the real clues to meaning might be.

The following box contains a number of unfamiliar words and some phrases that we don't often use in the same way now.

with respect to	much zeal	*named* mineral
some little care	very much	Hemipterous
(Zygaena)	Cicindela	White's 'Selborne,'
took much pleasure	simplicity	gentleman

a Read the following extract from the autobiography of the famous naturalist Charles Darwin.

Without worrying about the *missing words*, decide:

What do I learn about Darwin as a boy from the text?

Write a short paragraph in clear statement sentences presenting your thoughts.

………… science, I continued collecting minerals with …………. but quite unscientifically—all that I cared about was a new …………, and I hardly attempted to classify them. I must have observed insects with …………, for when ten years old (1819) I went for three weeks to Plas Edwards on the sea-coast in Wales, I was …………. interested and surprised at seeing a large black and scarlet …………. insect, many moths …………, and a …………. which are not found in Shropshire. I almost made up my mind to begin collecting all the insects which I could find dead, for on consulting my sister I concluded that it was not right to kill insects for the sake of making a collection. From reading '………….', I …………. in watching the habits of birds, and even made notes on the subject. In my …………. I remember wondering why every …………. did not become an ornithologist.

Adapted from Charles Darwin, *The Autobiography of Charles Darwin*

b Look back at the box of unfamiliar words and phrases. Decide which word or phrase fits into each of the spaces above.

c Now look at the paragraph you wrote about Charles Darwin as a boy. Are your statements still valid?

The chances are that **all** of the basic meaning you were able to work out from the text has come from the vocabulary that was most familiar to you.

d Try this technique for yourself. Read the next sentence from Darwin's autobiography and then using the technique, add any extra points to your paragraph about Darwin as a boy.

> Early in my school days a boy had a copy of the 'Wonders of the World,' which I often read, and disputed with other boys about the veracity of some of the statements;
> and I believe that this book first gave me a wish to travel in remote countries, which was ultimately
> fulfilled by the voyage of the *Beagle*.

3 Develop the skills

In dealing with unfamiliar concepts, it is important to use your powers of self-questioning that you learned about for Paper 1.

Treat each text like a puzzle and use some 'stop and think' questioning techniques to help you.

You will understand more than you think, once you do some **inferential reading**.

a Look at the following **task**.

What do you understand about Charles Darwin's favourite hobby as an older boy?

Use the student's 'stop and think' questions in the annotations on the extract to help you understand the text. Make notes on your ideas.

In the latter part of my school life I became passionately fond of shooting; I do not believe that any one could have shown more zeal for the most holy cause than I did for shooting birds. How well I remember killing my first snipe, and my excitement was so great that I had much difficulty in reloading my gun from the trembling of my hands. This taste long continued, and I became a very good shot. When at Cambridge I used to practise throwing up my gun to my shoulder before a looking-glass to see that I threw it up straight. Another and better plan was to get a friend to wave about a lighted candle, and then to fire at it with a cap on the nipple, and if the aim was accurate the little puff of air would blow out the candle. The explosion of the cap caused a sharp crack, and I was told that the tutor of the college remarked, "What an extraordinary thing it is, Mr. Darwin seems to spend hours in cracking a horse-whip in his room, for I often hear the crack when I pass under his windows."

Shooting? Does he mean criminal or sporting?

In that case, what sort of 'sport'? Who does that?

What's a snipe? I need to look back to the previous sentence for a clue.

The town or the university – what do I think?

Why is he doing this here? Doesn't he have a party to go to? What image have I got of him?

He's doing what?! Isn't this dangerous? Does this add to the image of the time?

Why does the tutor call him that? And who has a horse-whip anyway? Does this also give a picture of the time?

④ Final task

Now use all three extracts and the information and understanding you have gained from the activities to answer the following task.

What do you understand about Charles Darwin when he was young from the extracts in his autobiography?

Checklist for success

Remember that any successful comprehension response follows this basic pattern:

- clear **statements** in your own words addressing the question directly
- support for those statements with selected **quotations**
- using **inferences** to show your understanding.

Working with challenging sentences in 19th century texts

You are learning to:
- explore some techniques for dealing with the sentence structures of unseen 19th century texts
- develop your knowledge of punctuation to help you read unseen 19th century texts more confidently.

Testing: AO1, AO2, AO3
For: Paper 2 Section A

① Getting you thinking

Dealing with unfamiliar sentence structures can be a challenge. When you read older texts, particularly those from the 19th century, you often have to 'unpack' some very difficult, complex sentence structures.

A **complex sentence** still has, at its core, a **simple sentence**. However, it develops the idea contained in the simple sentence known as the main **clause**. It adds more detail and information in subsections known as subordinate clauses as they can't make sense alone, without the main clause.

a Make a copy of these three sentences. In each case, label the main clause and any subordinate clauses you can identify.

- The moon shone brightly.
- The moon shone brightly, lighting the pathway ahead through the woods.
- The moon shone brightly, lighting the pathway ahead through the woods, dappling the ground to make her journey less fearful, less foolish.

Key terms

complex sentence: develops ideas in a simple sentence and adds detail and information in subsections known as subordinate clauses

simple sentence: presents one idea. It will have one verb or verb phrase and contain one action, event, or state

clause: the basic part of a sentence containing a noun together with a verb, for example, 'The boy ran.'

② Explore the skills

The main punctuation marks we find in complex sentences are listed in the following chart. Examples of them are given in both creative and non-fiction writing.

a Read the definitions and then practise using the punctuation marks by completing the chart.

	Definition	In fiction	In non-fiction
comma	To separate the main clause from the subordinate clauses		As well as always being on their phones, teenagers play computer games, many of which are totally unsuitable.
semicolon	To join together two main clauses which have a link, instead of a conjunction	The train grudgingly pulled out of the station; we were going to war.	
pairs of commas, pairs of dashes (parenthesis)	Used to add an explanation or an afterthought into a sentence		Adults often complain about teenagers – though they were once teens themselves – and seem to have forgotten what a difficult time it can be.
colon	Used to introduce an explanation, description or list related to what has come before	Peterson checked out the room, mentally recording all he could see: burnt CDs, recording equipment, laptop and fresh milk on the counter. Someone had been here recently.	

It is important to read and use the clues in the punctuation to identify the main idea in each sentence. In that way, you can break down lengthy, complex sentences into their key ideas.

b Look at this final extract from Darwin's autobiography and make a list in note form of the key idea or ideas in each of the sentences in your own words. They have been numbered to help you. Use your notes to write a summary of what you learn from the extract about Darwin at school.

Think back

Remember to use all of the techniques you learned in Week 16, Lesson 1 to help you deal with unfamiliar vocabulary and from Week 15, Lesson 2 to help you write an effective summary.

Towards the close of my school life, my brother worked hard at chemistry, and made a fair laboratory with proper apparatus in the tool-house in the garden, and I was allowed to aid him as a servant in most of his experiments. [1] He made all the gases and many compounds, and I read with great care several books on chemistry, such as Henry and Parkes' 'Chemical Catechism.' [2] The subject interested me greatly, and we often used to go on working till rather late at night. [3] This was the best part of my education at school, for it showed me practically the meaning of experimental science. [4] The fact that we worked at chemistry somehow got known at school, and as it was an unprecedented fact, I was nicknamed "Gas." [5] I was also once publicly rebuked by the head-master, Dr. Butler, for thus wasting my time on such useless subjects; and he called me very unjustly a "poco curante," and as I did not understand what he meant, it seemed to me a fearful reproach. [6]

③ **Develop the skills**

Punctuation can be used in a complex way in 19th century texts, just like vocabulary, but it *is* designed to create pauses as you read.

Imagine each of the complex sentences being read aloud by your favourite actor!

Think of the punctuation marks as being their 'stage directions'.

When reading long complex sentences for yourself, it is useful to follow these 'stage directions' for the punctuation marks.

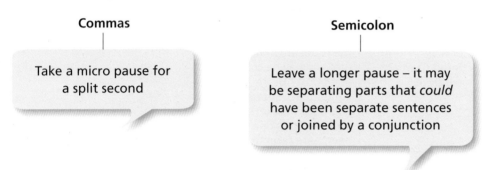

Commas

Take a micro pause for a split second

Semicolon

Leave a longer pause – it may be separating parts that *could* have been separate sentences or joined by a conjunction

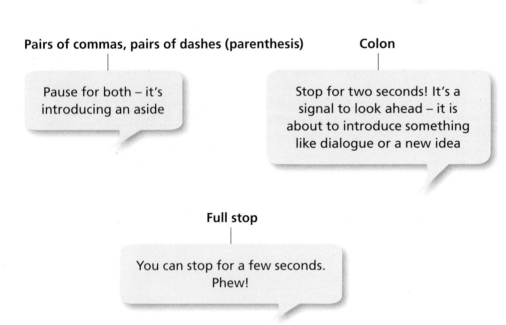

Pairs of commas, pairs of dashes (parenthesis)

Pause for both – it's introducing an aside

Colon

Stop for two seconds! It's a signal to look ahead – it is about to introduce something like dialogue or a new idea

Full stop

You can stop for a few seconds. Phew!

ⓐ Try reading aloud this extract from *Sketches by Boz* by Charles Dickens, written in the 1800s, where he describes watching a man in a London park. Use the 'stage directions' above to help you.

We were seated in the enclosure of St. James's Park the other day, when our attention was attracted by a man whom we immediately put down in our own mind as one of this class. He was a tall, thin, pale person, in a black coat, scanty gray trousers, little pinched-up gaiters, and brown beaver gloves. He had an umbrella in his hand – not for use, for the day was fine – but, evidently, because he always carried one to the office in the morning. He walked up and down before the little patch of grass on which the chairs are placed for hire, not as if he were doing it for pleasure or recreation, but as if it were a matter of compulsion, just as he would walk to the office every morning from the back settlements of Islington. It was Monday; he had escaped for four-and-twenty hours from the thraldom of the desk; and was walking here for exercise and amusement – perhaps for the first time in his life. We were inclined to think he had never had a holiday before, and that he did not know what to do with himself. Children were playing on the grass; groups of people were loitering about, chatting and laughing; but the man walked steadily up and down, unheeding and unheeded his spare, pale face looking as if it were incapable of bearing the expression of curiosity or interest.

Charles Dickens, from *Sketches by Boz*

b Make a list in note form of the key ideas about the man in the park that you can gather from the passage.

c Without repeating any of the words from the passage, make three inferences about the man. What is implied or suggested in Dickens' writing about this man?

④ Final task

Using the techniques you have learned, re-read the extract above, and then write a response to this comprehension task.

What do we understand about the man in St James's Park from the extract?

Checklist for success

- Use clear statements in your own words addressing the question directly.
- Support your statements with selected quotations.
- Use inferences to show your understanding.

Developing comprehension and synthesis skills

You are learning to:
- read with understanding, selecting the right information from both modern and 19th century texts
- show your understanding of what you read by selecting quotations from both texts
- make inferences to show your understanding of both texts
- gather your ideas from both texts into a response.

Testing: AO1
For: Paper 2 Question 2

① Getting you thinking

When working with a pair of challenging texts, it is helpful to begin with the most familiar or most contemporary text. This gives you a starting point for working with the second text.

a Read this contemporary text extract from *The New York Times*.

Source A

You need to see London at night, particularly the theaters. But not just the night life. London itself looks best in the dark. It's a pretty safe city, and you can walk in most places after sunset. It has a sedate and ghostly beauty. In the crepuscular kindness, you can see not just how she is, but how she once was, the layers of lives that have been lived here. Somebody with nothing better to do worked out that for every one of us living today, there are 15 ghosts. In most places you don't notice them, but in London you do. The dead and the fictional ghosts of Sherlock Holmes and Falstaff, Oliver Twist, Wendy and the Lost Boys, all the kindly, garrulous ghosts that accompany you in the night. The river runs like dark silk through the heart of the city, and the bridges dance with light. There are corners of silence in the revelry of the West End and Soho, and in the inky shadows foxes and owls patrol Hyde Park, which is still illuminated by gaslight.

AA Gill, from 'My London, and Welcome to it', *The New York Times*, 27 April 2012

Look at the following comprehension task.

> **What do you learn about the atmosphere in London from Source A?**

b Collect your ideas about the atmosphere in London and your supporting quotations. Then answer the question in a grid similar to the one below.

In Source A, I learn the atmosphere in London is...	Evidence from the text
• safe and secure • quiet, mysterious and lovely • • • • • •	'can walk in most places after sunset' 'has a sedate and ghostly beauty'

② Explore the skills

a Now write up two of the ideas you have collected in your grid. The example below will help to remind you of your method for presenting your comprehension skills to help you reach the Level 3 mark band.

The atmosphere in London is presented to us as being safe and secure and a place where you 'can walk in most places after sunset', which in some ways is different to our view of a modern day city after dark as they are often portrayed as dangerous.

— Select key information and present in a **statement**.

— Support your idea with evidence in a **quotation**.

— Demonstrate your understanding with an **inference**.

However, when showing your understanding of two texts, you need to be able to **synthesise** information quickly.

Key term

synthesise: draw together information from one or more sources

b Go on to read this second extract, from *Picturesque Sketches of London Past and Present,* by Thomas Miller, written in 1852.

Source B

There is something startling in the appearance of a vast city wrapt in a kind of darkness which seems neither to belong to the day nor the night, at the mid-noon hour, while the gas is burning in the windows of long miles of streets. The greatest marvel, after all, is that so few accidents happen in this dim, unnatural light, in the midst of which business seems to go on as usual, and would do, we believe, were the whole of London buried in midnight darkness at noonday, which would only be looked upon as a further deepening of the overhanging gloom. The number of lighted torches which are carried and waved at the corners and crossings of the streets add greatly to the wild and picturesque effect of the scene, as they flash redly upon the countenances of the passengers, and, in the distance, have the effect of a city enveloped in a dense mass of smoke, through which the smouldering flames endeavour in vain to penetrate.

During a heavy fog many accidents occur on the river, through barges running foul of each other, or vessels coming athwart the bridges; for there is no seeing the opening arch from the rock-like buttress, as the whole river looks like one huge bed of dense stagnant smoke, through which no human eye can penetrate. If you lean over the balustrades of the bridge, you cannot see the vessel which may at that moment be passing beneath, so heavy is the cloudy curtain which covers the water.

Thomas Miller, from *Picturesque Sketches of London Past and Present*

In order to write an effective response to both texts, it is important to:

- ask yourself what is different about the way London is presented in **both** sources

- organise that information logically and clearly.

c Look at this examination task.

> **Question 2:**
>
> **The way the writers present the city of London in darkness is different.**
>
> Use details from both sources to write a **summary** of the differences. **(8 marks)**

One effective way to gather your ideas is by using contrasting lists like the ones below to group the differences.

d Copy and complete the lists, adding in any further ideas of your own.

The ideas in your contrasting lists will form the basis of your clear statements in answering the question.

> *List 1:*
> *London seems like a kind of fictional, fairytale place*
>
> *List 2:*
> *London is a potentially dangerous place*
> *London is a place where you can't tell day from night*

③ Develop the skills

A further way to pull key ideas together is to consider quotations
which link to the same topic or idea – even if they deal with it in a
different way.

a Look at the quotations below from Source A, then find a
'partner' quotation from Source B which deals with the
same or a similar idea. The first one has been done as
an example.

Source A	Source B
1) 'It's a pretty safe city, and you can walk in most places after sunset.'	'The greatest marvel, after all, is that so few accidents happen in this dim, unnatural light'
2) 'It has a sedate and ghostly beauty.'	
3) 'The river runs like dark silk through the heart of the city'	
4) 'the bridges dance with light'	
5) 'inky shadows'	
6) 'still illuminated by gaslight'	

b For each pair of quotations you have collected, make notes
on what is suggested by each pairing in relation to the
contrasting presentation of London.

c Now look at this example of how a student has put
together their statements, quotations and inferences
on two texts in a clear and fluent way to respond to the
examination question in 2c.

> AA Gill states that London has a 'sedate and ghostly beauty' about it, which
> makes the city seems like a romantic place, a place which is not quite real
> and suggests somewhere quiet, mysterious and lovely. Miller also presents
> London as being supernatural in that the city is 'wrapt in a kind of darkness
> which seems neither to belong to the day nor the night'. This sounds less than
> romantic and suggests London in 1852 was more menacing and threatening
> than it is today.

d Write up a paragraph presenting one of your own ideas
from Activity 2a, supported by details or direct quotations
from your pairing exercise above and including your
inferences.

④ Final task

Using the techniques you have learned for comparing two texts, complete the following examination task.

> **The way the writers present the city of London in darkness is different.**
>
> Use details from both sources to write a summary of the differences. **(8 marks)**

Checklist for success

* Review the ideas from your contrasting lists and your quotation pairs.
* Write up three separate ideas.
* Use quotations to support each idea.
* Make inferences to show your understanding and to complete the task.

Applying comprehension and synthesis skills to Paper 2 Question 2

You are learning to:
- understand the mark scheme for Paper 2 Question 2
- practise your skills in reading both a modern text and a 19th century text carefully
- plan and write an examination task step by step.

Testing: AO1
For: Paper 2 Question 2

① Getting you thinking

a Take a look at this extract from the Question 2 mark scheme.

Note down:

- how the ladder of skills reflects the comprehension method you have been practising
- the most noticeable difference in moving from Level 2 to Level 3.

Level 3 Clear, relevant **5–6 marks**	Shows clear synthesis and interpretation of both texts: • Makes clear inferences from both texts • Selects clear quotations relevant to the focus of the task • Statements show clear differences/similarities between texts
Level 2 Some, attempts **3–4 marks**	Shows some interpretation from one/both texts: • Attempts some inference(s) from one/both texts • Selects some appropriate quotations from one/both texts • Statements show some difference(s)/similarity(ies) between texts

② Explore the skills

a You are now going to begin your planning for the following examination task.

These texts show us that the issues surrounding homelessness are different in the present than they were in the past.

Use details from **both** sources to write a summary of the differences. **(8 marks)**

Read the following sources carefully.

Source A is from a broadsheet newspaper published recently.

Sleeping rough for charity hides the real homelessness crisis

Organising a sponsored sleep-out is a preferred strategy for many homelessness charities up and down the country.

Jollies under the stars, making a mattress from cardboard and bedding down – these Bear Grylls excursions just perpetuate the myth that homelessness is about rough sleeping, and is therefore a much smaller problem than it really is.

The truth is that rough sleeping is the tip of the iceberg. It doesn't begin to cover the extraordinary scope of homelessness. Each year, homelessness affects around 400,000 people.

Imagine if 'experiencing homelessness' was sold to you as it really is. Most homeless people do not sleep in the street. You would most likely be sofa surfing, squatting, staying in hostels or being passed around B&Bs by the local council.

During this period you would also now be three times more likely to go to hospital, 13 times more likely to be a victim of violence and 47 times more likely to be victims of theft. One in five would have been robbed. Your life-span would be reduced from a healthy 81 years to just 47.

Since 2007, running a hostel for homeless people has been completely unregulated. Some landlords are fair and generous, but many force tenants to wallow in unhygienic conditions. 'Worse than prison,' is how one charity key worker I know described conditions in some London hostels.

Long spells in these hostels are common-place. One in 10 will stay for more than two years, most will stay for 12 months. If you don't like the conditions, or feel threatened, a refusal to take the option excludes you from any housing support in the future. Yet 8,000 people each year still take this course of action.

[…]

Every one of the 70,000 people in this hostel system is stuck in a grim and dangerous situation.

Tens of thousands more homeless live in filthy squats, far out of reach of help.

[…]

Hundreds of thousands more float from sofa to sofa, the legion of 'hidden homeless.' This problem is widespread. Rough sleeping is not. Society needs to understand how bad a situation we are really in.

Alastair Sloan, *The Guardian*, 29 October 2013

Source B is an extract from a 19th century non-fiction text,
Sketches by Boz, by Charles Dickens.

It is nearly eleven o'clock, and the cold thin rain which has been drizzling so long, is beginning to pour down in good earnest; the baked-potato man has departed – the kidney-pie man has just walked away with his warehouse on his arm – the cheesemonger has drawn in his blind, and the boys have dispersed.

The constant clicking of **pattens** on the slippy and uneven pavement, and the rustling of umbrellas, as the wind blows against the shop-windows, bear testimony to the inclemency of the night; and the policeman, with his oilskin cape buttoned closely round him, seems as he holds his hat on his head, and turns round to avoid the gust of wind and rain which drives against him at the street-corner, to be very far from congratulating himself on the prospect before him.

The little chandler's shop with the cracked bell behind the door, whose melancholy tinkling has been regulated by the demand for quarterns of sugar and half-ounces of coffee, is shutting up. The crowds which have been passing to and fro during the whole day, are rapidly dwindling away; and the noise of shouting and quarrelling which issues from the public-houses, is almost the only sound that breaks the melancholy stillness of the night.

There was another, but it has ceased. That wretched woman with the infant in her arms, round whose meagre form the remnant of her own scanty shawl is carefully wrapped, has been attempting to sing some popular ballad, in the hope of wringing a few pence from the compassionate passer-by. A brutal laugh at her weak voice is all she has gained. The tears fall thick and fast down her own pale face; the child is cold and hungry, and its low half-stifled wailing adds to the misery of its wretched mother, as she moans aloud, and sinks despairingly down, on a cold damp door-step.

Charles Dickens, from *Sketches by Boz*

Glossary

pattens: clogs

b Now go on to gather your three key ideas for the examination task.

As you plan, remember to:

- ask yourself what you learn from the texts about homelessness, past and present
- organise that information logically using a table or contrasting lists
- select partner quotations that you can use in support.

③ Develop the skills

a Look at the ideas you have collected so far. These will form the basis of your clear **statements** in response to the task.

Double check that your chosen **quotations** will support your ideas precisely.

You are now going to work on your **inferences**.

Plan ideas for your own inferences using sentence starters such as:

This suggests that…

This implies that…

From this we may infer that…

④ Final task

Using all of your notes and ideas, go on to write a complete answer for the examination task.

> **These texts show us that the issues surrounding homelessness are different in the present than they were in the past.**
>
> Use details from **both** sources to write a summary of the differences. **(8 marks)**

Checklist for success

- Make clear statements in your own words addressing the question directly.
- Support those statements with selected quotations.
- Make inferences to show your understanding.
- Remember this is an 8-mark short answer task.

Introducing language skills

You are learning to:
- understand some more language subject terminology relevant to non-fiction texts
- develop your knowledge about language and how to examine and analyse it
- develop your ability to comment on why language is used in certain ways and its effect on the reader.

Testing: AO2
For: Paper 2 Question 3

① Getting you thinking

Paper 2 is called 'Writers' viewpoints and perspectives' and the non-fiction sources on this paper will present a particular view on a theme or topic. As a result of this, the language features you will find in these texts will include those you studied for Paper 1, but they are also likely to include some specific techniques known as **rhetorical language features**.

a Recap these language features you learned about for Paper 1. Ensure you are clear about them and write down either an example or a definition of each.

> noun phrase   simile   metaphor   alliteration

Look again at the terms:

> viewpoint   perspective

Again, write your own clear definition of each key term.

> **Key term**
>
> **rhetorical language features:** language techniques designed to persuade a reader to consider an idea from a different point of view

② Explore the skills

a Now go on to re-read this text, which you are already familiar with, and look closely at the rhetorical devices the writer uses to persuade you to think about their **viewpoint**. Answer the questions in the annotations to develop your understanding.

Organising a sponsored sleep-out is a preferred strategy for many homelessness charities up and down the country.

Jollies under the stars, making a mattress from cardboard and bedding down (1) just perpetuate the myth that homelessness is about rough sleeping, and is therefore a much smaller problem than it really is.

The truth is that rough sleeping is the tip of the iceberg (2). It doesn't begin to cover the extraordinary scope of homelessness. Each year, homelessness affects around 400,000 people (3).

Imagine if 'experiencing homelessness' was sold to you as it really is. Most homeless people do not sleep in the street. You would most likely be sofa surfing, squatting, staying in hostels or being passed around B&Bs by the local council (4).

During this period you would also now be three times more likely to go to hospital, 13 times more likely to be a victim of violence and 47 times more likely to be victims of theft. One in five would have been robbed. Your life-span would be reduced from a healthy 81 years to just 47 (5).

Since 2007, running a hostel for homeless people has been completely unregulated. Some landlords are fair and generous, but many force tenants to wallow in unhygienic conditions. 'Worse than prison,' is how one charity key worker I know described conditions in some London hostels (6).

[…]

Tens of thousands more homeless live in filthy squats, far out of reach of help. Hundreds of thousands more float from sofa to sofa, the legion of 'hidden homeless.' This problem is widespread. Rough sleeping is not. Society needs to understand how bad a situation we (7) are really in.

Alastair Sloan, *The Guardian*, 29 October 2013

(1) Look at this combination of three different aspects to think about. Known as a **list of three** or a **triplet**, it is often found in persuasive writing. Why do you think this technique has such an impact?

(2) What does this well-known phrase (which is also a **metaphor**) imply?

(3) The writer uses a **statistic** here – a measurement or a number – presented as a blunt fact. What effect does this have?

(4) Note how this paragraph speaks to 'you' as a reader. This is known as **direct address**. What does this make you imagine?

(5) Which different **rhetorical devices** you have met so far are used again in this paragraph?

(6) Look at the way a **comparison** is made in this paragraph and is given greater effect by the use of a **quotation** from a trusted source. How would this add weight to the writer's viewpoint?

(7) Yet more statistics in this paragraph but note at the end the writer includes all of us by using 'we'. This is known as an **inclusive pronoun**. How does it make you feel?

Key terms

statistic: when numbers or figures are used in a text as factual evidence

direct address: when a writer uses the words 'you' or 'your' to make it seem like they are speaking to you personally

inclusive pronoun: using 'our' or 'we' to make it feel like we have a shared viewpoint or responsibility.

③ Develop the skills

As you discovered when working on language for Paper 1, identifying the language features is just one step towards showing your skill and meeting the assessment objective.

Once again, you need to think about the effect or impact those features might have on a reader.

a Look at this example from a student dealing with the metaphor in paragraph 3.

> The journalist uses a metaphor 'the tip of the iceberg' to describe rough sleeping. This implies that people who sleep rough are only a tiny part of the problem and issue of homelessness. It makes me imagine that there are other vast problems associated with homelessness that are maybe hidden or out of sight, suggesting much more needs to be done to tackle the problem.

— language feature

— example

explains why the metaphor is there and what it is doing

clearly explains a possible effect on the reader (the student)

develops to think about why the feature is effective

The student has not only explained the metaphor clearly, but has also shown what its impact and effect is in a **developed** way.

b Look back at your notes from Activity 2 and choose a different feature to work with. Write a paragraph in which you:

- identify the feature
- quote the example
- explain what it is doing
- explain what it makes you think of, feel or imagine.

④ **Final task**

Using all of your notes from Activity 2, try this examination task. Aim to use your new terminology and to develop your comments on effect.

> **How does the writer, Alistair Sloan, use language to make you, the reader, think about the problems related to homelessness?** (12 marks)

Checklist for success

- In this response, select no more than three language features.
- Make sure you give an example of each one.
- Make a comment that explains what the feature is actually doing.
- Develop your comment by deciding on what it makes you think of, feel or imagine.

Developing language skills

You are learning to:
- understand how creative language features can be used in non-fiction texts
- develop your knowledge of how to comment on those features in non-fiction texts
- develop your ability to comment on how those features might affect you, the reader.

Testing: AO2
For: Paper 2 Question 3

1 Getting you thinking

Exploring writers' language techniques means you focus on the craft of the writer and the range of ways they use language to communicate ideas to the reader. Writers of non-fiction can still use the kinds of **language special effects** you found in your study of fiction for Paper 1 to express their views and perspectives.

a Read this extract from *The Road to Wigan Pier*, where George Orwell uses a range of language techniques to express a particular viewpoint.

A slag-heap is at best a hideous thing, because it is so planless and functionless. It is something just dumped on the earth, like the emptying of a giant's dust-bin. On the outskirts of the mining towns there are frightful landscapes where your horizon is ringed completely round by jagged grey mountains, and underfoot is mud and ashes and overhead the steel cables where tubs of dirt travel slowly across miles of country. Often the slag-heaps are on fire, and at night you can see the red rivulets of fire winding this way and that, and also the slow-moving blue flames of sulphur, which always seem on the point of expiring and always spring out again. Even when a slag-heap sinks, as it does ultimately, only an evil brown grass grows on it, and it retains its hummocky surface. One in the slums of Wigan, used as a playground, looks like a choppy sea suddenly frozen; 'the flock mattress', it is called locally. Even centuries hence when the plough drives over the places where coal was once mined, the sites of ancient slag-heaps will still be distinguishable from an aeroplane.

George Orwell, from *The Road to Wigan Pier*

b Can you match the following language features with the highlighted areas of the extract?

- **simile**
- **alliteration**
- **personification**

c Choose one of the techniques and write a short paragraph in your own words explaining why you think Orwell has used it, and what effect you think it creates.

Think about:

- the mood or atmosphere being created
- how particular words/phrases make you feel
- the image created by particular words/phrases.

Key terms

simile: form of comparison using 'as' or 'like'

alliteration: repetition of a sound, usually (but not always) at the start of a sequence of words

personification: a type of metaphor where an inanimate object is given human characteristics such as emotions

(2) Explore the skills

a Look at the following example of a student's response to this activity.

> Orwell uses the simile 'like a giant's dust-bin' to suggest that the slag-heap is enormous and disgusting. It makes the reader imagine a huge heap of rubbish, and creates a kind of monstrous feeling to the picture with the use of the word 'giant'. It suggests that this amount of waste is out of human control.

identifies the correct technique and uses the right terminology

evidence is embedded into the student's sentence

comments on effect by exploring what it makes the reader imagine and feel

develops the effect by thinking about what the simile does

b Now read the next section of the text. Find one example each of the techniques:

- simile
- metaphor
- personification.

> At night, when you cannot see the hideous shapes of the houses and the blackness of everything, a town like Sheffield assumes a kind of sinister magnificence. Sometimes the drifts of smoke are rosy with sulphur, and serrated flames, like circular saws, squeeze themselves out from beneath the cowls of the foundry chimneys. Through the open doors of foundries you see fiery serpents of iron being hauled to and fro by redlit boys, and you hear the whizz and thump of steam hammers and the scream of the iron under the blow.

A student has identified the metaphor: 'fiery serpents of iron' from the text. They have gone on to think about the **connotations** of this metaphor.

c Look at their ideas below:

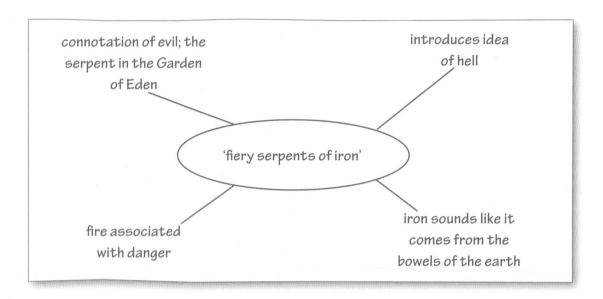

connotation of evil; the serpent in the Garden of Eden

introduces idea of hell

'fiery serpents of iron'

fire associated with danger

iron sounds like it comes from the bowels of the earth

d Create two more spider diagrams exploring the connotations of the:

- simile
- use of personification

that you identified earlier in this lesson.

③ Explore the skills

Another of the techniques Orwell uses in this passage is **a semantic field** of danger. A **semantic field** is a group or collection of words that link to one topic or idea. They create similar **connotations** in the mind of the reader. For example, the words 'gun', 'trench', 'battlefield', 'tank' in a text create a semantic field of war.

a Read the passage again and make a list of all the words and phrases Orwell uses that have suggestions or **connotations** of danger.

b What is Orwell suggesting to you about how it must **feel** to live and work there through his use of this **semantic field**? What does it make you **imagine**?

Key term

connotations: the associations and connections we make when we think about particular words. For example, the connotations of the word 'red' might include love, passion, danger, fire or heat

④ Final task

Now you have read the extracts and identified some of the ways language techniques are being used, you are ready to form a response to a question.

> **How does Orwell use language techniques to suggest that the industrial north of England is a dangerous, unhealthy place to live?**
>
> Select two or three specific features in order to create a more developed response. You don't have to write about everything.

Checklist for success

- Select no more than three language ideas or special effects.
- Make sure you give an **example** of each one.
- Make a comment that explains the effect of the example by deciding on what it makes you **think of**, **feel** or **imagine**.

Applying language skills to Paper 2 Question 3 using a modern source

You are learning to:
- understand how the examination question works
- work step by step through an examination question, practising the method
- consider a student response and the mark scheme
- write up a complete response.

Testing: AO2
For: Paper 2 Question 3

① Getting you thinking

a Look closely at the type of language task you will be given on Paper 2. It is different to the format of the task on Paper 1. The notes will help you understand the task thoroughly.

> You now need to refer only to Source A, Jessica Ennis' description of preparing to win an Olympic gold medal. (from lines… to the end)
>
> **How does Ennis use language to make you, the reader, feel the tension and excitement of her Olympic experience?**
>
> **(12 marks)**

You will be asked to focus on one of the sources, either A or B.

You will be given some information about the topic.

You will be given a specific part of the text to focus on. This will be a much longer extract than in Paper 1.

The question here reminds you to think about the effect on *you*.

There are 12 marks for this question, so a longer and more detailed response is required compared to Paper 1.

You should aim to spend 15–20 minutes planning and writing for this task.

② Explore the skills

Now you are going to plan for the examination task given above.

a Read the extract below carefully. It is from the autobiography of Jessica Ennis. In it, she describes the moments before her first big event in the London 2012 Olympics.

> This is the day that I have dreamt about for years. This has been what all that dying on the side of a track has been about. This is the end of the raging pain. This is my one opportunity. My one shot. Walking into this arena is an assault on the senses – the purple and green and red, the crescendo of noise and the haze at the end of the straight where the Olympic flame is burning bright. This is it. This is my chance. I cannot help thinking that if it all goes wrong I will never get this opportunity again. I might make another Olympics, but it won't be at home and I won't be touted as the face of the Games again.

This combination of circumstances will never arise again. It is my first time and my last chance. Finally I realize just how big and scary the Olympic Games are. I follow the other girls to the start and we get into our blocks. It's like that Eminem song goes: one opportunity to seize everything you want. Will I capture the moment or let it slip? It has taken me sixteen years to get here. Now I have seven events and two days to make it all worthwhile. There have been countless times when I have wondered if it would happen. I have been down, broken and almost out, but I have dragged myself back from the brink. Part of me wonders how this has happened. I am just an ordinary girl from a run-of-the-mill street in Sheffield and yet I have been plucked out of that normality and plunged into this melting pot of hopes and dreams and fierce competition. It is what I have wanted when I have been training every day, but it is frightening.

I feel adrenaline, excitement and fear. I have lost my crowns in the last year and there are bigger, stronger girls ready to push me around. Tatyana Chernova is the world champion. Nataliya Dobrynska is the Olympic champion. I have no titles, just one shot. We crouch and the roar drops to total silence. It is that special moment of bated breath and possibility. And then suddenly, in those seconds before the gun, I feel a strange calmness wash over me and I am ready. It is now or never.

Jessica Ennis, from *Unbelievable*

b Now make some notes on the writer's language choices using the questions below to help you.

1) Look closely at paragraph 1:

- What seems to be important about the use of personal pronouns in this paragraph?

- Can you find a metaphor used for effect?

- Can you see any examples of listing or rhetorical questions?

- Which words or phrases in particular help to show her nervousness?

2) Look again at paragraph 2:

- Why do you think she uses so many numbers here?
- What does she want you to realise with the phrases 'ordinary girl' and 'run-of-the-mill street'?

3) Finally look again at paragraph 3:

- Can you see a list of three used?
- How many words are connected to feelings and atmosphere?

c From your notes, select **four** language features or ideas. Write them down and make a note of their **examples**.

③ Explore the skills

You have now collected the features and examples you will focus on in your response.

You are going to move on to develop your comments on effect.

a Look at this student response with its examiner comments.

- Identify the areas of this answer that could be improved to make it match the checklist on the right.
- Rewrite the paragraph with your own suggested improvements.

> **Think back**
>
> In Week 18, you learned that you should:
>
> - identify the feature
> - quote the example
> - explain what it is doing
> - explain what it makes you think of, feel or imagine.

> Jessica Ennis uses a lot of language features in this extract. She describes the event as 'an assault on the senses – the purple and green and red, the crescendo of noise and the haze at the end of the straight… is burning bright.' This sentence has a lot of adjectives and also some listing and also some alliteration. This makes it seem very busy and bright and noisy with a lot going on.

Examiner comment:

There is an awareness of language here, and the use of some terminology (adjectives, listing, alliteration). However, a whole sentence is used as the example, so it is very difficult to see if the candidate really knows what each of these terms mean. There are no specific examples. There is one very simple and generalised comment on the effect of the language. All Level 1.

Level 1	Shows simple awareness of language:
Simple, limited	• Offers simple comment on effect
1–3 marks	• Selects simple examples or textual details
	• Makes simple use of subject terminology, not always appropriately

b Prepare your own comments on effect for each of your four chosen language features. Make some notes on:

- what the feature is actually doing or contributing to the piece of writing
- what the feature is making you think of, feel or imagine.

④ Final task

You are now going to put together your full response to the examination task, using your selected features and examples from Activity 2 and your notes from Activity 3.

> **How does Ennis use language to make you, the reader, feel the tension and excitement of her Olympic experience?**
>
> **(12 marks)**

Checklist for success

- In this response, select no more than four language features.
- Make sure you give an example of each one.
- Make a comment that explains what the feature is actually doing.
- Develop that comment by deciding on what it makes you think of, feel or imagine.

Applying language skills to Paper 2 Question 3 using a 19th century source

You are learning to:
- practise an examination task step by step
- think about the mark scheme skills
- develop your ability to plan your response
- consider a student response to evaluate your own work.

Testing: AO2
For: Paper 2 Question 3

① Getting you thinking

a Reflect on each of the final tasks you have completed for Paper 2, Question 3. Use the mark scheme to identify their strengths and weaknesses.

Level 3 Clear, relevant **7–9 marks**	Shows clear understanding of language: • Explains the effects of language choices clearly • Selects a range of relevant examples • Makes clear and accurate use of subject terminology
Level 2 Some, attempts **4–6 marks**	Shows some understanding of language: • Attempts to comment on the effect of language • Selects some appropriate examples • Makes some use of subject terminology, mainly appropriately

② Explore the skills

Your language question for Paper 2 may ask you to focus on Source A: the modern text from the 20th or 21st century or Source B: the text from the 19th century. This may be because the language in the older text is more descriptive or has more opportunities for you to work with than the modern one in that particular pairing.

a Using your skills in reading 19th century texts from Week 16, carefully read the text below. It is a piece of journalism reporting on a visit to Newgate Prison in London.

> **Think back**
>
> The response you looked at in Week 19, Lesson 1, Activity 3 was a Level 1 response. Refresh your memory of the ladder of skills for answering language questions by looking at the mark scheme on the left.
>
> Note that the numbers of marks for this question are different to Paper 1. In total, there are 12 marks for Paper 2 Question 3. This is to reflect that you have a much longer extract to work with and more selection to do yourself.

In the first apartment into which we were conducted were five-and-twenty or thirty prisoners, all under sentence of death – men of all ages and appearances, from a hardened old offender with swarthy face and grizzly beard of three days' growth, to a handsome boy, not fourteen years old, and of singularly youthful appearance even for that age, who had been condemned for burglary.

[…]

A few paces up the yard, lie the condemned cells. […] all the prisoners under sentence of death are removed from the day-room at five o'clock in the afternoon, and locked up in these cells, where they are allowed a candle until ten o'clock; and here they remain until seven next morning.

We entered the first cell. It was a stone dungeon, eight feet long by six feet wide, with a bench at the upper end, under which were a common rug, a bible, and a prayer book. An iron candlestick was fixed into the wall at the side; and a small high window in the back admitted as much air and light as could struggle in between a double row of heavy, crossed iron bars. It contained no furniture of any description.

Conceive the situation of a man, spending his last night on earth in this cell. Buoyed up with some vague and undefined hope of reprieve, he knew not why – indulging in some wild idea of escaping, he knew not how – hour after hour of the three preceding days has fled with a speed which no man living would deem possible, for none but this dying man can know.

[…]

Hours have glided by, and still he sits upon the same stone bench with folded arms, heedless alike of the fast, decreasing time before him […] The feeble light is wasting gradually, and the deathlike stillness of the street without, broken only by the rumbling of some passing vehicle which echoes mournfully through the empty yards, warns him the night is waning fast away. The deep bell of St Paul's strikes – one! He heard it; it has roused him. Seven hours left! He paces the narrow limits of his cell with rapid strides, cold drops of terror starting on his forehead, and every muscle of his frame quivering with agony.

Charles Dickens, from *Sketches by Boz*

b Look at the following examination task.

You now need to refer only to Source B, Dickens' description of a visit to Newgate Prison.

How does Dickens use language to make you, as a reader, imagine the experiences of the prisoners? **(12 marks)**

c A student has begun to gather ideas for the task in a table below. Complete the table by locating some correct examples of each feature.

Types of language feature I have noticed:	Examples I could use:
noun phrases	a hardened old offender
personification	
interesting verbs	
semantic field of time	five o'clock seven next morning hour after hour
a metaphor	

③ Develop the skills

a Using the table, select four of the features you feel most confident in writing about.

Plan your comments for each feature by thinking about:

- what the feature is actually doing or contributing to the piece of writing
- what the feature is making you think of, feel or imagine.

b Go on to write up your complete response to the examination task in no more than 15 minutes.

(4) Final task

(a) Look at this sample student response to the task and the examiner's annotations.

Dickens uses a variety of noun phrases in the text to ———— correct term + examples
describe the prisoners themselves such as 'a hardened
old offender' and 'a handsome boy'. These help us to see
the contrast between the prisoners and the different ———— explains use of noun phrase
ages that are put together. This makes me feel shocked
as a boy of fourteen today would never be put in prison or
sentenced to death for burglary and helps me to see how ———— explains effect on reader
unjust some of their experiences are.

The writer also creates a semantic field of time by making ——— correct term + a number
references to the times of the day, 'five o' clock', 'ten of examples
o' clock', 'seven next morning' for those condemned to
death. This gives a sense of the time passing and makes ———— explains use of semantic
me imagine the fear and the horror of waiting for a death field
sentence, knowing those 'hours and hours' are your ——— explains effect on reader
last ones. very thoughtfully

This fear is emphasised by the use of the metaphor 'cold ——— correct term + example
drops of terror' which I think is referring to cold sweat
on the prisoner's brow. Again this makes me imagine explains use of metaphor
the physical feelings of the prisoners and their fear and – we know the student
anxiety as they wait for death with no escape. understands it

another clear comment on
the effect for reader

(b) Using the mark scheme from Activity 1 decide if your
response is:

- stronger than
- weaker than
- similar to

the example. Is there anything you can learn from the
example to help you improve your own technique?

Half-term progress assessment task: Paper 2 Questions 1 and 2

You are aiming to show that:
- you can read an unseen non-fiction text carefully and with understanding, picking out the right types of information
- you can read both modern and 19th century texts carefully and with understanding, picking out the right types of information
- you can support your ideas on those texts by being able to select quotations from both texts
- you can make inferences about what things might mean or suggest to you to show your understanding of both texts.

Testing: AO1
For: Paper 2 Questions 1 and 2

What you can expect in the exam

In Paper 2 Section A of the exam, you will be asked to read two pieces of source material, both of which are non-fiction. One will be from the 20th or 21st century and the other will be from the 19th century. You are unlikely to have seen the passages before.

Your job is to apply your skills of reading and analysis to the questions about the passage. You have **one hour** to read and complete **four questions** worth **40 marks** – half of the marks for Paper 2. In this test you will work on Questions 1 and 2.

Step 1

Begin by reading the extract below carefully. It is taken from the autobiography of Steve Backshall, an explorer and natural history TV presenter, written in 2011. In it, he describes a journey on a river with his film crew in Papua New Guinea.

Source A

> As if to prove the doubters right, that very afternoon I was running the Zodiac out from a small creek on to the main river, and the engine stalled and stopped dead. As I frantically tried to restart it, yanking on the starter cord,
> 5 our little boat got caught up in a furious whirlpool at the mouth of the creek, and all hell broke loose. It got spun round and round in dizzying circles, and on each turn the side was dragged under water and brown river poured in. Pretty soon we were up to our knees.

10 I abandoned the engine and took up my paddle, frenziedly
trying to pull us out of the maelstrom, as the folks in the
other boat yelled and screamed at us from outside the
whirlpool. [...] Finally, the rapid spat us out and we were
cast off downstream, dragged under a rocky overhang,
15 then out into the rapids again. Relieved, I breathed out and
flopped down in the boat, but the other boat was yelling
again: 'PADDLE, BLOODY PADDLE, STEVE!' I looked up,
saw that we were passing the safety of a rocky bank, and
just beyond it downstream was a fierce rapid that could
20 spell danger. I struck for shore, and at the last moment
jumped out into the flow and dragged the boat to safety.

[...]

The mood in the camp is quite sombre as we continue
packing for our journey downstream. The foreboding of
25 the doubters has spread, and some of the crew honestly
think they may never see us again. For a while the tension
infects me too, and I find myself anticipating the worst.

[...]

Somewhat inevitably, we head off downriver prepared
30 for a hellride we might never return from. In the event,
it turned into a fabulous cruise through one of the most
beautiful prehistoric environments I'd ever seen. Maybe
six miles downstream of basecamp was as far as anyone
had ventured before, so we immediately felt as if we were
35 blazing a trail into the wilderness. The shallow forested
slopes prevalent around basecamp soon disappeared,
as the river plunged into a gorge with vertical limestone
cliff faces a hundred metres high on both sides. Massive
waterfalls plunged down into the river every hundred
40 metres or so, creating vast clouds of spray billowing up
into the sunlight.

[...]

Every one of the waterfalls is spectacular enough that if
it were in Europe people would travel hundreds of miles
45 to see it. Here in the forests of New Guinea there are
hundreds, sometimes four or five down one riverside in the
space of a couple of hundred metres. It is one of the most
awe-inspiring places, truly a wonder of the world.

The promised terror-ride though, couldn't have been less
50 in evidence. All our lifelines, lifejackets and secured
equipment looked totally over the top as we roared
through that paradise on our outboard-driven dinghies.
I'd had scarier drives down to Tesco.

Steve Backshall, from *Looking for Adventure*

Step 2

Now read your first examination task and write out your answer carefully. This is testing your basic skills for AO1.

Question 1:

Look again at the section highlighted in yellow.

Choose four statements below that are TRUE.

Choose a maximum of four statements.   **(4 marks)**

a) Steve stopped dead as he was sailing out of the creek.

b) Steve took his boat out onto the main river.

c) The boat was turning round fast in a whirlpool.

d) Steve remained very calm as he tried to start the boat's engine.

e) When Steve flopped down in the boat, he was out of danger at last.

f) The river flooded the boat up to their knees.

g) The people in the other boat had to drag Steve's boat to safety.

h) Steve had to use a paddle to try to get out of the swirling water.

Step 3

When you are happy with your response, move on to the next task. This is also testing your skills for AO1.

Read the second piece of source material carefully (Source B). It is taken from *Travels in West Africa*, a collection of travel writing by the Victorian woman explorer Mary Kingsley, published in 1897. Here she writes about her journey down the Ogowé River in West Central Africa.

Source B

On we paddled a long way before we picked up village number one, mentioned in that chart. On again, still longer, till we came to village number two. Village number three hove in sight high up on a mountain side soon after, but it was getting
5 dark and the water worse, and the hillsides growing higher and higher into nobly shaped mountains, forming, with their forest-graced steep sides, a ravine that, in the gathering gloom, looked like an alley-way made of iron, for the foaming Ogowé. Village number four we anxiously looked for; village number
10 four we never saw; for round us came the dark, seeming to come out on to the river from the forests and the side ravines, where for some hours we had seen it sleeping, like a sailor with his clothes on in bad weather. On we paddled, looking for signs of village fires, and seeing them not.

15 [...]

About 8pm we came to a corner, a bad one; but we were unable to leap on to the bank and haul around, not being able to see either the details or the exact position of the said bank, and we felt, I think naturally, disinclined to spring in the direction
20 of bits of country as we had had experience of during the afternoon.

[...]

About 9.30 we got into a savage rapid. We fought it inch by inch. The canoe jammed herself on some barely sunken rocks
25 in it. We shoved her off over them. She tilted over and chucked us out. The rocks round being just awash, we survived and got her straight again, and got into her and drove her unmercifully; she struck again and bucked like a broncho, and we fell in heaps upon each other, but stayed inside that time.

30 [...] We sorted ourselves out hastily and sent her at it again. Smash went a sorely tried pole and paddle. Round and round we spun in an exultant whirlpool, which, in a light-hearted, maliciously joking way, hurled us tail first out of it into the current.

35 [...]

Unpleasant as going through the rapids was, when circumstances took us into the black current we fared no better. For good all-round inconvenience, give me going full tilt in the dark into the branches of a fallen tree at
40 the pace we were going then – and crash, swish, crackle and there you are, hung up with a bough pressing against your chest, and your hair being torn out and your clothes ribboned by others, while the wicked river is trying to drag away the canoe from under you.

45 [...]

Our eyes, now trained to the darkness, observed pretty close to us a big lump of land, looming up out of the river. This we subsequently found out was Kembe Island. The rocks and foam on either side stretched away into the
50 darkness, and high above us against the star-lit sky stood out clearly the summits of the mountains of the Sierra del Cristal.

Mary Kingsley, from *Travels in West Africa*

Step 4

Complete:

Question 2:

You need to refer to Source A and Source B for this question.

The experience of both writers in their boats is similar.

Use details from both sources to write a summary of the similarities. **(8 marks)**

Checklist for success

- Make clear statements in your own words, addressing the question directly.
- Support those statements with selected quotations.
- Make inferences to show your understanding.
- Remember this is an 8-mark short answer task.

Half-term progress assessment task: Paper 2 Question 3

You are aiming to show that:
- you can show knowledge about the choices of language and language features used in a given text and the effect those choices have on you, the reader.

Testing: AO2
For: Paper 2 Question 3

Step 1

This task tests your skills for AO2 – identifying and commenting on the use of language in the text and its effect. Read the question carefully and note how many marks are available to you.

> **Question 3:**
>
> You now need to refer only to Source B, Mary Kingsley's description of travelling by canoe on the Ogowé River.
>
> **How does Mary Kingsley use language to make you, the reader, feel the danger and tension of her experience?**
>
> **(12 marks)**

Step 2

Now carefully re-read lines 24 to 55 in the extract from Source B, which deals with Mary Kingsley's description of travelling by canoe.

Step 3

Plan your response using a table similar to the one below.

Language feature	Examples I could use

Step 4

Write your response in no more than 15 minutes, then check your work carefully.

Checklist for success

- Select four language features, giving an example of each.
- Explain what the feature is doing.
- Develop your comment by explaining what it makes you think of, feel or imagine.

Check your progress: Section A

Grade 8

- I can summarise and critically evaluate with detailed and perceptive understanding.
- I can understand and respond with insight to explicit and implicit meanings and viewpoints.
- I can analyse and critically evaluate detailed aspects of language, grammar and structure.
- I can back up my understanding and opinions with judicious references and supporting quotations.
- I can make convincing links between texts.

Grade 5

- I can summarise and evaluate with accuracy and clear understanding.
- I can understand and make valid responses to explicit and implicit meanings and viewpoints.
- I can analyse and evaluate relevant aspects of language, grammar and structure.
- I can support my understanding and opinions with sensibly chosen references to texts.
- I can make sensible links between texts.

Grade 2

- I can describe and summarise with some accuracy and understanding.
- I can respond in a straightforward way to most explicit information and viewpoints.
- I can make some relevant comments about language and structure.
- I can support my comments and opinions with some general references.
- I can make straightforward links between texts.

Introducing viewpoint and perspective

You are learning to:
- recognise how different viewpoints can be presented on the same topic
- explore how the same techniques can be used to present both viewpoints
- begin to gather your own viewpoints on a chosen topic.

Testing: AO6 and AO7
For: Paper 2 Question 5 and your Spoken Language Endorsement

1 Getting you thinking

Whether we are thinking about climate change or status updates, people often have very different viewpoints.

a What different viewpoints can you think of about whether or not schools or companies should have a uniform? Think about price, quality, individuality, and a sense of belonging.

b Which viewpoint do you think might be held by schools, a student, a teacher or a parent, or by a company, an employee and a customer? Explain why.

Presenting your viewpoint in a formal way is a life skill and one that you will need to use both in Paper 2 for your Section B: Writing and to help you achieve a strong outcome for your Spoken Language Endorsement.

2 Explore the skills

a Read the following article and then answer the questions below to help you think about how the viewpoint here is presented.

Why I'm taking my child out of school for a holiday

This half-term, my family and I are leaving the country for a much-needed break. To save around £800, I will be taking my child out of school before the term officially ends. I have not sought permission from the head teacher. Nor will I.

[...]

Firstly, I genuinely don't feel my child (aged 4) will be disadvantaged by one or two days out of school. Second, and controversially, I don't feel the school will be disadvantaged either. I know how the argument goes – if everyone behaved like me we'd be in a sorry state with half-empty classrooms. But, really, would we? Aren't those who shout the loudest about the need for attendance the ones who are rich enough for term-time holidays never to be an issue?

I do feel guilty, but only for families who don't have the same financial resources as we do, so can't have a holiday at all, term time or not. I can't imagine any teacher devaluing the chance to learn a few words of a foreign language in situ, to see geology in action by playing on black sand, or start to understand basic engineering principles by looking at how planes fly. For us, the physical, intellectual and social advantages of travel would not be financially possible if we waited until the school holidays. Of course, I agree that attendance (most of the time) is vital but so is family harmony, unfrazzled parents, time to read or explore the world without the pressures of day-to-day life. Until travel companies offer more reasonable prices during school holidays, families like mine will continue to take their children out of school. Perhaps we should go easy on parents who value spending time with their children in a new and stimulating environment over Ofsted attendance targets.

Anonymous, *The Guardian*, 29 January 2014

1. What is the writer's view on taking children out of school in term time?

2. Make a list of all of the reasons the writer gives to explain their viewpoint.

3. How does the writer include and engage you in their argument? Do you sympathise or agree with them at any point?

4. Can you see any rhetorical language features in the article? Choose one and note down how it helps to strengthen the message.

5. Can you identify any sentences that have been used to add impact or dramatic effect? Which ones bring you up short, for example, and force you to pause and think?

6. What sort of **tone** does the writer take in their argument?

7. Decide whether you agree or disagree with the writer and make a list of three reasons justifying why or why not.

Key term

tone: links to the idea of 'tone of voice'. It suggests a sound quality or 'voice' in the text that is speaking to you in a particular way

③ Develop the skills

a Now look at this second article, which takes the opposite viewpoint to the first article. Read it carefully and make some notes about what is **similar** in the way this writer **presents** her viewpoint.

You might think about:

- openings and conclusions
- use of reasoning
- use of opinions
- use of rhetorical questions
- use of a friendly, but formal tone
- use of varied sentences for effect/dramatic pause.

Why I'll never take my children out of school for a holiday

As chief holiday-planner in our household of six, I could be a lot richer – and/or my children could have seen a lot more of the world – if I'd fished them out of school, or even just shaved a few days off the beginning or end of term here and there. Instead, over the last 16 years while we've had school-age kids, we've kept our holidays religiously within the vacation dates: and as my youngest child is still only 11, we've got another seven years of the same ahead.

It's irksome, because there are huge financial savings to be made. Also, who wants to be on the beach in August, when it's packed and baking hot, when June and September [...] are so less crowded, and the temperature more agreeable?

So why not just flout the system? Well, it all comes down to respect. Like all parents, I have occasional issues with aspects of my children's education: but on the whole, I aim to respect and support the primary and comprehensive schools where they are, and have been, pupils. [...]

So many parents seem not to realise that the reason their kids don't work hard, or play truant, or get into trouble with their teachers, is connected to the fact that they have an a la carte attitude to rules themselves. If you want your child to stick two fingers up at their teachers, to think education doesn't matter, or to skimp on revising for an exam, then go ahead and take them out of school so you can jet off on an exciting holiday for a fortnight. What you are role-modelling by your behaviour is your belief that rules are for other people, not for you; and your kids will pick up on that very, very quickly.

And here's another thing. My eldest, post-uni, is currently saving up to go to Asia on a gap year. Because travel is for life; but school is only for childhood, and as holiday-loving parents we need to remember that.

Joanna Moorhead, *The Guardian*, 29 January 2014

④ Final task

Choose one of the statements below. On a mind map, plot five clear reasons why you either agree or disagree with the statement. An example has been done for you.

1. Young people are far too young to be able to get married at 16.

2. Young people should definitely be able to vote at the age of 16.

3. Allowing young people to learn to drive a car at the age of 17 is reckless and dangerous.

4. Teenagers are far too young at the age of 14 to be studying for exams that are so important for their futures.

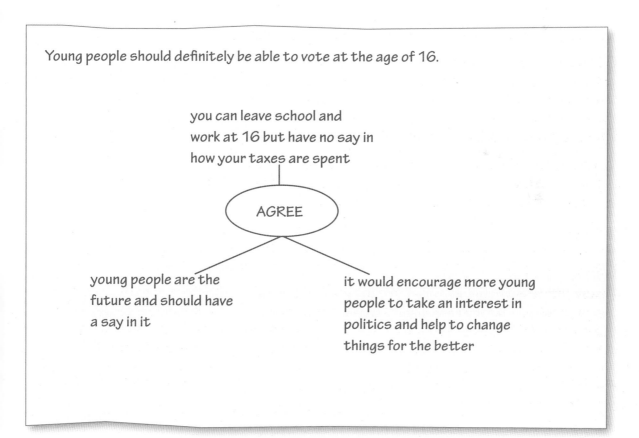

Young people should definitely be able to vote at the age of 16.

you can leave school and work at 16 but have no say in how your taxes are spent

AGREE

young people are the future and should have a say in it

it would encourage more young people to take an interest in politics and help to change things for the better

Planning a formal presentation expressing your own viewpoint

You are learning to:
- explore the key skills of informing, explaining and persuading
- select an appropriate task of your own choice which will use two of those purposes
- plan ideas for a presentation using a five-point structure with topic sentences
- consider appropriate language features to include in your presentation.

Testing: AO7 and AO6
For: Spoken Language Endorsement and preparation for Paper 2 Question 5

1 Getting you thinking

Your Spoken Language Endorsement is based on you delivering a formal presentation. It is a good way to demonstrate your skills in speaking confidently. Planning for a presentation is just the same as planning for a piece of writing. As your presentation needs to be formal and on a topic of your choice, it is also a good way to help you prepare for Paper 2 Question 5.

The first step is to choose your topic and the type of presentation you feel most comfortable delivering.

- Will you feel more comfortable explaining to others about something you know a lot about, for example, art or computer games?

- Do you feel confident in persuading others of your viewpoint about a serious issue, for example, global warming?

a Look at the short extracts below, each of which is written with a different **purpose** in mind. Which text is **informing** you, which text is **explaining** and which one is **persuading** you? How do you know? Make some notes to justify your choices.

A

> The garden faces south and is approximately thirty metres long. It has a number of large trees for shade but is generally in direct sunlight all day. There are a number of fruit trees and an old garage desperately in need of repair. The soil in this area is mainly clay and so quite heavy.

Key terms

purpose: the 'job' a piece of writing is doing, for example, narrating, describing, persuading

informing: telling your reader about something; presenting them with crisp, clear factual information

explaining: unpicking something for your reader and making it clear; presenting reasons and helping your reader understand something

persuading: getting a reader on your side and sharing your views or attitudes

B

When I want to escape from the stresses of everyday life, I love nothing more than to get out into my garden, a hobby I never thought I'd ever take up. Being outside in the fresh air gives me time out from work and the kids and I always feel better, even after just an hour.

C

Have you ever thought about getting stuck in down at your local community allotment with a trowel or a fork? It's great fun and a good way to get out in the fresh air, get some exercise and meet new people. You could be part of a team that's actually putting something back into the community and there are lots of projects and events at the allotment for all ages.

(2) Explore the skills

a Make a start on planning your own presentation by selecting one of the task choices below. Think carefully about the choice you make. Ensure that you then select for yourself a topic that you are knowledgeable about or willing to research.

Either:

Choose a hobby, sport or interest that you feel passionately about. Write a **formal presentation** in which you **inform** your audience about your chosen topic and **explain** why you love it.

Or:

Choose an issue which is close to your heart or that you feel very strongly about. Write a **formal presentation** in which you **inform** your audience why this issue is so important and **persuade** them to share your point of view.

b Write out a **statement** confirming the topic of your presentation and its purpose(s): inform, explain and/or persuade.

c Create a mind map where you plot your five key ideas or viewpoints as you did in the Final task of Week 21, Lesson 1.

For example:

> A presentation explaining my love of gardening
>
> or
>
> A presentation persuading my listeners that we should do more locally to care for the environment.

d Now, just as you did when you were planning for an effectively structured piece of writing for Paper 1, you are going to write topic sentences for each of your five ideas. You could organise them in a table like this:

Ideas for explanation/Reasons for viewpoint	Topic sentence
Para 1: First started gardening to get out of the house/escape stress/work/kids	Gardening always seemed like a chore, but now, I think it is the ideal way to combat stress and relax.
Para 2: Fresh air and exercise	
Para 3: Knowledge and skills built up	
Para 4: Satisfaction of growing own things	
Para 5: Hobby could lead to a new career	

③ Develop the skills

Now you have a way of structuring the ideas for your presentation and strong statements to begin each paragraph that you write. You are going to gather some interesting **rhetorical language features** to **persuade** your listener or some key **explanatory** features to engage your listener.

a Look at these two example paragraphs. Which one is the strongest and why?

A

> Dustbins left overflowing in back alleys, litter on every street, chewing gum on pavements. Is this really the way we want our local environment to look? I'm really passionate about the place where I live. I've lived here for twelve years now. There's a strong community and it's a friendly neighbourhood but we really don't do enough about caring for the place as a team.

B

> I am really unhappy with how our local environment looks. I think people just don't care enough really and I'm totally sick of it. It's an eyesore around all the terraces with all the litter and all the bins that no one can be bothered putting out. Really, people are just lazy round here.

Think about the following.

- Which one has made a more engaging impression on the audience?
- Which one feels more reasoned and formal in its tone?
- Which one has used more interesting features?

b For each of your planned paragraphs, select at least one feature from the **Informative box** below.

Add it to your planning notes with a written example.

Think back

If you are unsure of some of these terms, then think back to Week 18 where you were learning about these terms and their effects.

Informative box of tricks

facts	statements	adjectives to create a
opinions	proper nouns	specific picture
statistics	subject specific words	

---

c Now add in features from either the **Persuasive** or the **Explanatory box**, depending on which task you chose.

Persuasive box of tricks

direct address
rhetorical questions
lists of three
inclusive pronouns
statistics
use of simile or metaphor

Explanatory box of tricks

reasoning
facts
personal opinion
direct address
listing
anecdotes
comparisons

---

④ Final task

Write up the first draft of your formal presentation.

Key term

anecdotes: mini stories which add weight to the point you are making

Checklist for success

- Organise your draft into five paragraphs.
- Begin each paragraph with your topic sentence.
- Include at least one interesting feature in each paragraph.

Developing your formal presentation

You are learning to:
- think about what makes a spoken presentation engaging
- use examples from speechmakers to create an effective opening
- explore effective techniques to engage your audience and conclude your presentation
- re-draft your work and organise it into note form.

Testing: AO7 and AO8
For: Spoken Language Endorsement (and preparation for Paper 2 Question 5)

① Getting you thinking

When you are a student, you see presentations every day: in the form of a teacher or lecturer giving a lesson. So, what makes a good lesson?

a Put these statements in order of importance:
- a topic that is really interesting
- a teacher who knows what they are talking about
- a teacher who uses complex terms you are unfamiliar with
- hand-outs with key information
- a supporting PowerPoint that the teacher just reads out from.

b What can you learn, by looking at your list, about giving your own presentation?

② Explore the skills

Now you can work on your presentation and consider the most effective way to present it. The first thing to think about is your opening and how strong it will be for your listeners.

a Read Hillary Clinton's introduction to her speech about women's rights. Answer the questions in the annotations.

A

> This is truly a celebration, a celebration of the contributions women make in every aspect of life: in the home, on the job, in the community, as mothers, wives, sisters, daughters, learners, workers, citizens and leaders.

How does Hillary Clinton make a positive start? Why might this be important?

What does this list do? Does it leave any woman out?

It is also a coming together, much in the way women come together every day in every country. We come together in fields and factories, in village markets and supermarkets, in living rooms and board rooms. […] We come together and talk about our aspirations and concerns. And time and again, our talk turns to our children and families. However different we may appear, there is far more that unites us than divides us.

Hillary Clinton, American Rhetoric, www.americanrhetoric.com/speeches/hillaryclintonbeijingspeech.htm

How does she use this comparison to connect with her audience?

What patterns do you notice here?

What is the impact of this strong statement? How convincing is it?

Key term

register: the choice of vocabulary, grammar and style you make for your audience, for example, formal or informal

b Now read this second extract, which uses a completely different **register** for a different audience. It was given by American Navy Admiral William McRaven to students graduating from university. Again, make notes on the questions in the annotations.

B

It's been almost 37 years to the day since I graduated from the University of Texas. I remember a lot of things about that day. I remember I had a throbbing headache from a party the night before. I remember I had a serious girlfriend, whom I later married and I remember that I was getting commissioned in the Navy that day.

But of all the things I remember, I don't have a clue who the commencement speaker was that evening, and I certainly don't remember anything they said. So, acknowledging that fact, if I can't make this commencement speech memorable, I will at least try to make it short.

The University's slogan is 'What starts here changes the world.' I have to admit – I kinda like it. 'What starts here changes the world.' Tonight there are almost 8,000 students graduating from U.T. That great paragon of analytical rigour, Ask.Com, says that the average American will meet 10,000 people in their lifetime. That's a lot of folks. But, if every one of you changed the lives of just 10 people – and each one of those folks changed the lives of another 10 people – just 10 – then in five generations – 125 years – the class of 2014 will have changed the lives of 800 million people.

William McRaven, University of Texas News, http://news.utexas.edu/2014/05/16/mcraven-urges-graduates-to-find-courage-to-change-the-world

How does McRaven make a connection with his student audience?

How is he engaging those students who may not be listening to him?

This is a formal speech but he uses a slightly less formal register. Why do you think that is?

What is the impact of the use of the statistics here? How might they make his audience think about their future?

c Look back at the introduction to your own speech and redraft it. Make improvements by asking yourself these questions.

- Have I made a positive start to engage my audience?
- Am I using the right register to address the group I am speaking to?
- Am I involving my audience by using inclusive pronouns or direct address?
- Could I use some listing or comparison for effect?
- Could I use some interesting facts or statistics to really make my audience think and take them by surprise?

③ Develop the skills

The end of your presentation also has to have a lasting impact on your audience for maximum, convincing effect.

a Look at the endings below of the two speeches. While the speeches are on different topics, there are similarities. Note down three similarities in the techniques used by each speechmaker to create a strong conclusion. You could begin:

> Both speechmakers use...to leave the audience with...

A

As long as discrimination and inequities remain so commonplace everywhere in the world, as long as girls and women are valued less, fed less, fed last, overworked, underpaid, not schooled, subjected to violence in and outside their homes – the potential of the human family to create a peaceful, prosperous world will not be realized.

Let – Let this conference be our – and the world's – call to action. Let us heed that call so we can create a world in which every woman is treated with respect and dignity, every boy and girl is loved and cared for equally, and every family has the hope of a strong and stable future. That is the work before you. That is the work before all of us who have a vision of the world we want to see – for our children and our grandchildren.

B

> But, YOU are the class of 2014, the class that can affect the lives of 800 million people in the next century.
>
> Start each day with a task completed. Find someone to help you through life. Respect everyone.
>
> Know that life is not fair and that you will fail often. But if you take some risks, step up when the times are toughest, face down the bullies, lift up the downtrodden and never, ever give up – if you do these things, then the next generation and the generations that follow will live in a world far better than the one we have today.
>
> And what started here will indeed have changed the world – for the better.

b Redraft your own conclusion to leave a strong message, trying out some of the techniques used by Clinton and McRaven.

④ Final task

Now reduce and summarise your presentation onto **cue cards** so you are not tempted to just 'read out' your presentation.

> *Gardening presentation Card 2 of 4*
>
> <u>Fresh air and exercise</u>
>
> – stop me being a couch potato
>
> – don't need to go to the gym
>
> – healthy, e.g. vitamin D from sunlight
>
> – doing something for the environment

Key term

cue cards: small note cards used by speakers and presenters with key reminders of what they are going to say

Checklist for success

- Use a different card for each paragraph of your speech.
- Head up each card with your topic sentence.
- List key points from each paragraph on your card.

Introducing point-of-view forms and conventions

You are learning to:
- explore some of the main forms you may be asked to write in for Paper 2 Question 5
- understand some of the key techniques and features of those forms.

Testing: AO5
For: Paper 2 Question 5

① Getting you thinking

For Paper 2 Question 5, you will be asked to write a text in which you present your own point of view. You are expected to write in way that shows your view and perspective using an appropriate register. You are therefore likely to be given a **form** such as a letter, a speech or an article. There are a number of **conventions** that guide the way you write each of those forms.

Key terms

form: category or types of texts that have similar characteristics

conventions: the kinds of features that are often found or associated with a particular form

a Each of the following forms has particular conventions, so the language features shown are likely to be different in each case. Can you match the text in each case to the language examples?

1. Letter to your local MP arguing logically for improved transport for young people between the ages of 11 and 16.

2. Opinion article expressing your feelings about bad fashion/clothing decisions.

3. Speech to your classmates urging them to take personal responsibility for their local environment.

Openings

As I walk down the street and take a look around me, some days I am incredulous…

Dear Sir/Madam,

I'd like to talk to you about something I feel strongly about…

Middle sections

On the one hand, it is true that… yet, on the other, it is clear…

Another key reason I feel we need to change our behaviour is…

The industry itself sells an image that is unrealistic and based on profits…

Endings

> Yours faithfully
>
> So next time you part with your hard-earned cash for the latest look, think twice.
>
> Thank you for listening, and I hope what I have said gives you food for thought.

② Explore the skills

The **conventions of speeches** mean they are often used to call for change or to persuade the audience to do or believe something. This may lead to the use of more rhetorical devices and emotive or powerful language to create an impact.

In this speech from 1852, former slave Frederick Douglass addressed citizens of his hometown, Rochester, USA, about the injustice of slavery.

a Read the extract and then identify:

- references to the audience (and the speaker himself)
- examples of emotive imagery or vocabulary
- repetition or patterns used for impact
- a clear statement of the purpose of the speech – what needs to change
- any other features you would expect to see in persuasive speeches of this nature.

> Whether we turn to the declarations of the past, or to the professions of the present, the conduct of the nation seems equally hideous and revolting. America is false to the past, false to the present, and solemnly binds herself to be false to the future. Standing with God and the crushed and bleeding slave on this occasion, I will, in the name of humanity, which is outraged, in the name of liberty, which is fettered, in the name of the Constitution and the Bible, which are disregarded and trampled upon, dare to call in question and to denounce, with all the emphasis I can command, everything that serves to perpetuate slavery – the great sin and shame of America!
>
> Frederick Douglass, 'What to the slave is the fourth of July?', 5 July 1852

③ Develop the skills

In a similar way to speeches and your presentation, the conventions of **opinion editorials/articles** are that they often reflect on recent issues or events, and establish a familiar tone with their reader to get them on side.

Key term

op-ed article: an article or essay in a newspaper, expressing the opinions or viewpoint of a writer who does not work for that newspaper

a Read this extract from an **op-ed article** which takes a viewpoint on the issue of modern slavery.

The well-dressed couple at Sheffield railway station decline to take a leaflet from The Salvation Army volunteer raising awareness about **modern slavery**. "No thank you," they say. "Slavery doesn't happen here. Not where we live."

The truth is different. Slavery is everywhere – today, across modern Britain, in backstreets and upmarket suburbs alike. It is likely that the same couple encounter the victims of this appalling crime every day, without realising it. [...]

That couple might be dining out at a smart restaurant where the potatoes on their plates were picked by men who earn little or nothing, often bound by a "debt" to their trafficker, and sleep in groups in freezing shipping containers. [...]

Our couple's glasses may have been washed by a vulnerable young woman whose manager gives her leftovers from customers' plates but no money. Their taxi home may have just dropped off men at an upmarket brothel offering British girls for sale.

Sound far-fetched? "Sadly, it's not," says Major Anne Read, The Salvation Army's anti-trafficking response co-ordinator. "Although hypothetical, those scenarios are just the kind of thing happening throughout every region in the UK. It really is that close to us all."

Julia McCaffrey, *The Telegraph,* 31 October 2014

---

b What language devices or features does this article use which fit with the conventions of **op-ed articles**? Find examples of the following:

- use of both formal and informal language
- use of an anecdote or imagined scenario
- use of listing for rhetorical effect
- use of inclusive pronouns to include the reader in a shared view.

Letters will be personal, but the conventions of formal and informal letters mean that the language and features will change accordingly. In this formal example, a young woman sends a letter to her MP calling for more action on modern slavery in her local community.

c Read the letter, then identify and make notes on:

- where and how the letter sets out or introduces the issue at hand
- the formal features of language used, such as choice of vocabulary
- the logical and explanatory language used to get her point across
- the 'call to action' which she suggests to the MP.

Dear Mr Malone,

I am writing to express my concerns about the possible issue of modern slavery in our community. We are a rural community with a number of seasonal workers who come and go through the summer months.

I have noticed over the past few weeks the poor state of some of these workers as I drive out to work each day and return late. Although I realise picking vegetables has to be done while they are fresh, the hours that workers are in the fields seems unreasonable. Additionally, workers are in a poor state of dress, look neglected and malnourished and I am very concerned that we have some seasonal workers in our community who are being exploited.

I would urge you to look into this matter and campaign for all employers in our area to show they are providing proper facilities for seasonal workers to be safe and healthy as well as ensuring they are being paid fairly for the work they do.

Yours sincerely

Lorna McCloud

4 Final task

Have a go at drafting a letter to your own MP in which you make a call for action on an issue which concerns you in your local area. You might think about: a proposed building development; a lack of facilities for children/young people/the elderly; the closure of an important facility such as a library.

Checklist for success

- Use the planning skills you have learned from organising your presentation: planning paragraphs with topic sentences.
- Use the conventions of the letter you read in Activity 3c.
- Aim to write approximately 200–250 words for this task.

Planning and structuring your viewpoints into writing

You are learning to:
- explore different ways of planning effectively for a point-of-view writing task
- consider how to organise your paragraphs using discourse markers
- explore some student responses
- plan and write part of a practice task in the familiar form of a speech.

Testing: AO5
For: Paper 2 Question 5

① Getting you thinking

Just as for planning your presentation, good organisation is the key to success when writing in the examination. Even though you may feel time is short, a plan helps you to stay focused in the time available. It helps you to organise your ideas and viewpoints in a much clearer and logical way.

 Read this task.

> In recent years, 'Gap Years' – a period when young people travel abroad before they go to college, or start a job – have become increasingly fashionable.
>
> Write an article for your college website in which you give your point of view about gap years, and whether they are a good idea.

A student has jotted down their plan for the article, as follows:

Approach 1

> Paragraph 1: Introduction
>
> <u>For</u>
>
> Paragraph 2: Need a break from studying and work
>
> Paragraph 3: Broadens your mind – meet new people, friends
>
> Paragraph 4: Use Gap Year to help others by volunteering

Against

Paragraph 5: Costs a lot of money – not fair to rely on parents

Paragraph 6: Doesn't really broaden your mind – it's just a holiday really

Paragraph 7: Can be dangerous, and you could get lonely

Paragraph 8: Conclusion

b What other ways could they have organised their plan?

② Explore the skills

There are several ways of organising your ideas when you wish to persuade your reader. You can also structure your ideas as follows.

Approach 2

Paragraph 1: Introduction

Paragraph 2: **For** – need a break from work, etc.

Paragraph 3: **Against** – costs a lot of money, etc.

Paragraph 4: **For**…etc.

Paragraph 5: **Against**…etc.

a How is this different from Approach 1?

b Now look at this third approach.

Approach 3

Although gap years can be incredibly expensive and most students will need financial support from parents or to undertake fundraising, it will be money well spent. After all, everyone needs a break from work to refresh their minds and bodies, and after being at school since the age of five it is money well spent if your travels help you consider your next step in life.

- What is the point of view of the writer? How do you know?
- Where are the 'for' and 'against' arguments here?
- How is this different from Approach 2?

There are different ways of introducing a counter argument.

You can include it in the first clause of your sentence, using words or phrases such as:

'While', 'Although', and 'Even though'

These words and phrases are known as **discourse markers** as they mark a shift in the tone, idea or topic of your piece of writing.

Or you can introduce it with phrases such as:

'Some people believe that…', and follow this with a **new sentence** beginning with a different discourse marker.

c Copy and complete the examples below using one of these approaches.

Select from the **discourse markers** in the box.

While	Although	Even though
Some people believe that		Some argue that
However	On the other hand	Nevertheless Yet

1. _____ travelling abroad for a long time could make you feel lonely, and there are many dangers you could face _____.

2. _____ a year out just makes you restless. _____, it could be said that you come back realising what is good about your home life, friends and family.

3. _____ travelling alone takes courage, some might say that it is less stressful when you only have yourself to look after.

③ Develop the skills

The style and length of your paragraphs can also create an impact on your reader.

a Read these final two paragraphs from one student's essay.

I know that everyone says that a year out is a precious experience and the memories will last forever, but, as far as I am concerned, the thing that will last the most is the debt! Volunteering overseas is incredibly expensive. I don't come from a rich family and university is going to cost me a lot anyway.

The truth is, the biggest 'gap' will be in my wallet.

- What is the writer's point of view?
- What is different about the two paragraphs?
- Why do you think the writer chose to end the essay in this way?

It is important to stick to a separate idea or point in each paragraph, but the information you select is key.

The average gap year will cost between £3000–£4000 – meaning that 22% of parents contribute to their child's travel, spending approximately £763 to help them, often more. The cost of the year can be even higher if the student does organised trips, or wants specialist experiences such as whale-watching or doing the Inca trail, things that can cost upwards of £500 alone.

However, such costs can create unforgettable memories, and enable students to do things they will never have a chance to do once they are in a job or married. Just imagine sitting in some dull office job, staring out at the rain and traffic, and wishing you had done something exciting while you could!

Information from Lattitudes website: http://www.lattitude.org.uk

- What has the writer included in the first paragraph to support their argument?
- How is the style and focus of the second paragraph different?

④ Final task

You have been asked to give a talk at your college on your views about whether it is a good idea for young people to take a break when they leave school or college before they go on to further study or to choose a career.

Plan your speech, deciding on approaches 1, 2 or 3. Write the first three paragraphs of your speech, using the approach you have chosen.

Checklist for success

- List your for/against points.
- Decide what sequence or order you wish to present your ideas in.
- Use a variety of paragraph styles to get your message across.
- Add different types of content to each paragraph.

Developing the structure of your viewpoints

① Getting you thinking

Once you have organised the overall paragraph structure of your response, you can strengthen and develop it by considering how you will link and build your ideas within those paragraphs. This is how professional journalists are able to achieve such fluency in their point-of-view writing.

a Read the opening to an article below by Hadley Freeman and make notes on the following.

- What is Hadley Freeman's main point of view in this article?
- Where, in the first paragraph, do we find this out?

Why black models are rarely in fashion

I unashamedly love fashion, but there is much for which the ———— topic sentence
fashion industry deserves to be to be criticised: the obsession
with skinniness, the **fetishisation** of youth, the **misogynistic**
promotion of fashion items that are, quite frankly, torturous (6in
heels, I'm looking at you). But the grotesque element in fashion
that I personally find the most **egregious** is its blatant racism. ———— specific focus on key issue
Black models never, with single-digit exceptions in a decade,
appear on the cover of major fashion magazines, because, as the
black model Jourdan Dunn told the Guardian last year, 'people
in the industry say if you have a black face on the cover of a
magazine it won't sell.' ———— supporting example

Glossary

fetishisation: an excessive obsession

misogynistic: woman-hating

egregious: outstandingly bad

- How does the second paragraph:

  – provide further evidence of her main viewpoint

  – subtly alter it?

> Then there are the fashion shows. Until this season it was by no means uncommon to go to a show and see only white models on the runway. Jezebel.com has charted the presence of models of colour at New York fashion week and there is no doubt there has been an improvement: at the shows this time six years ago, 87% of the models were white, 4.9% were black, 5.4% were Asian and 2.7% were Latina. This month the stats were, respectively, 78.69%, 7.67%, 9.75% and 2.12%. The shows in London have also shown an increased effort at acknowledging diversity, with special credit going to Burberry, Topshop and Tom Ford. Whereas several shows last season were all white, as the Sunday Times pointed out last weekend, this time none of them were.
>
> Hadley Freeman, *The Guardian*, 18 February 2014

second topic sentence

focus on the issue in relation to fashion shows

statistical evidence to support argument

② Explore the skills

The order of the **first paragraph** is key to both understanding Hadley Freeman's point of view, and to the impact she wants to make.

- The first sentence **sets the context** by explaining the writer's love of fashion and her understanding of some of the obvious things wrong with it.

- The second sentence, however, focuses in on the single **more serious, and perhaps surprising point she wants to make**.

- The third sentence hammers this home with a very **specific example to support the previous point**.

a Thinking back to the article above, why couldn't the order of these three sentences be changed? (For example, why couldn't the second sentence come first?)

b Re-order these three sentences on a similar issue into a new paragraph so that it works in the same way.

> This is especially true of the 'skinny' look; if young women didn't want it, why do they continue to buy into it? They are only reflecting what society seems to want in terms of body style. It is wrong to blame fashion magazines for promoting a particular look.

c Read Hadley Freeman's **second paragraph** again and answer these questions.

- How is the first sentence of the second paragraph different in style from the first sentence of the opening paragraph?
- How does it link back to the first paragraph?
- What is the structure of the second paragraph?
- What is the job of the first two sentences?
- What do sentences three, four, five and six add?

③ Develop the skills

Hadley Freeman links her sentences (and paragraphs) together to explain her point of view in a fluent way.

a Read this further extract and look at the highlighted words and phrases.

- How does the use of the **determiner** 'these' (1) link back to the previous sentences or paragraphs?
- How do the linking words or phrases, 'But', 'For a start' and 'Moreover' (2) help to guide us through her argument?

But (2) let's look at these (1) stats with standards that are slightly higher than a grasshopper's knee. For a start, (2) for American designers to choose more than three-quarters of their models from the Caucasian demographic is, to say the least, hardly reflective of the country. Some of those formerly all-white London shows, such as Paul Smith, cast a grand total of one black model and a whopping two Asian models. Insert slow applause. Moreover, (2) these (1) changes have only come about with heavy effort from the Council of Fashion Designers of America in the US and the British Fashion Council in the UK, which sends out letters every single season to designers specifically asking them to reflect London's diversity.

Key term

determiner: a word or phrase which indicates the distance between ideas or things in a text. For example, 'those books' (far away); 'these books' (close to hand)

b Look at this table. Select appropriate words or phrases, then copy and use them to complete the passage below.

pronouns/determiners (useful for referring back to previously mentioned items)	I, we, he, she, they, you, him, her, them, us this, these, that, those, such
words/phrases which explain contrasts	yet, but, however, on the other hand, in contrast
words/phrases which add to or stress a point	moreover, furthermore, also, in addition
words/phrases which give reasons or describe an effect	for example, as, in this way, thus, therefore, because
words/phrases that indicate sequence or time order	recently, later, firstly, secondly, finally, then, next, before that, now

_____treatment of black models is unacceptable. _____, it is probably illegal, as the same rights that apply in other professions should apply here. _____, how can you change things? If the industry is so misguided, then forceful action must be taken. _____ customers must boycott fashion brands. _____ we would then see a change, perhaps.

④ Final task

'The fashion industry is responsible for lots of society's problems.'

Write the first two paragraphs of an article for a lifestyle blog in which you explain your viewpoint on this issue.

Think about:

- how people of different colours and races are represented and treated
- how the use of very slim models affects us
- the use of young models.

Checklist for success

- Engage the reader with detailed, relevant ideas.
- Write clear paragraphs linked in a logical manner.
- Use a range of connecting words and phrases to signal and develop your point of view.

Working on varied sentences for effect

You are learning to:
- explore the impact that varied sentence structures can make using examples
- expand your knowledge of different structural techniques to vary sentences
- practise using varied sentence structures by improving a response.

Testing: AO5 and AO6
For: Paper 2 Question 5

① Getting you thinking

a Imagine you are a journalist and have been asked to write a 500-word **op-ed article** called 'Women and weight' for a national broadsheet lifestyle magazine.

What do you think of this as a starting point?

> I think that there is a real problem with women and weight in this country at the moment. Women are getting fatter all the time, and this is causing real health problems for the country. Forty years ago the average size was a size 10, and now it is a 16. Women are made to feel bad about this, and because of this they often hide their problem and become secret eaters, which only makes the problem worse.

> **Think back**
>
> Earlier in the course, in Week 5, you learned about how important varied sentence structures were to craft effects in creative writing. However, in point-of-view writing they are just as important to provide variety and interest for your reader. Once you have planned and linked ideas within your paragraphs, you can work at sentence level to add even more impact.

b Now read the first paragraph from 'Why I am fat!' by Caitlin Moran on the same subject.

> Why did I get fat? Why was I eating until I hurt and regarding my own body as something as distant and unsympathetic as, say, the state of the housing market in Buenos Aires? Obviously, it's not wholly advisable to swell up so large that, on one very bad day, you get stuck in a bucket seat at a local fair and have to be rescued by your old schoolmaster, but why is being fat treated as a cross between terrible shame and utter tragedy? Something that – for a woman – is seen as falling somewhere between sustaining a sizable facial scar and sleeping with the Nazis?
>
> Caitlin Moran, from *How to be a Woman*

c What is your response to this opening paragraph?

- Is it better than the first one? If so, why?
- What is Moran's viewpoint on being overweight?
- What kind of tone is being created in this introduction?
- How does the sentence structure vary from the first example to help create this tone?

② Explore the skills

a Look at this list of some of the structural techniques Moran uses in her first paragraph to create varied sentences and a lively tone. Identify an example of each:

- very short sentence
- **rhetorical questions**
- **hyperbolic questions**
- personal anecdote
- dashes to emphasise a particular idea (or ideas).

Moran uses personal **anecdotes** deliberately. In the article, the anecdote sounds as if it is just an example. Do you think it might have actually happened? If so, why does she not say this directly?

b Read the next paragraph of Moran's article. As you read, notice how she uses parentheses (brackets).

> Why will women happily boast-moan about spending too much ("...and then my bank manager took my credit card and cut it in half with a sword!"), about drinking too much ("...and then I took my shoe off and threw it over the bus stop!"), and about working too hard ("...so tired I fell asleep on the control panel, and when I woke up, I realized I'd pressed the nuclear launch button! Again!") but never, ever about eating too much? Why is unhappy eating the most pointlessly secret of miseries? It's not like you can hide a six-Kit-Kats-a-day habit for very long.

c What have the sections in parentheses got in common? What kind of tone do they help to create?

d How many rhetorical questions has Moran used in the first two paragraphs? What is the purpose of all the questions and how do they help to communicate her viewpoint successfully to the reader?

Key terms

rhetorical questions: questions which are designed to make the reader think, not to answer directly

hyperbolic questions: exaggerated questions designed to make particular points

anecdotes: mini stories which add weight to the point you are making

③ Develop the skills

a Now read the final three paragraphs of the article.

> Perhaps it's time for women to finally stop being secretive about their vices and instead start treating them like all other addicts treat their habits. Coming into the office looking frazzled, sighing, "Man, I was on the pot roast last night like you wouldn't believe. I had, like, MASH in my EYEBROWS by 10 p.m."
>
> Then people would be able to address your dysfunction as openly as they do all the others. They could reply, "Whoa, maybe you should calm it down for a bit, my friend. I am the same. I did a three–hour session on the microwave lasagna last night. Perhaps we should go out to the country for a bit. Clean up our acts."
>
> Because at the moment, I can't help but notice that in a society obsessed with fat—so eager in the appellation, so vocal in its disapproval—the only people who aren't talking about it are the only people whose business it really is.

b What is the difference between the tone at the start and at the end of the article? Which one is the more serious? Why do you think Moran has structured her text in this way?

④ Final task

Look at the extract on the following page from a student response to the task below set in Week 23, Lesson 2. Rewrite the response to create a more engaging tone by varying the sentence structures and using some of the techniques Caitlin Moran uses in her writing.

> **'The fashion industry is responsible for lots of society's problems.'**
>
> Write the first two paragraphs of an article for a lifestyle blog in which you explain your viewpoint on this issue.

The fashion industry is responsible for a lot of problems in today's society. I think one of the problems is it puts you under pressure to look a certain way. This means that you don't always feel comfortable in what you wear and sometimes the clothes people wear just do not suit them but they buy and wear them anyway just because they are in fashion.

This leads me to my next point which is money. Keeping up with fashion costs a a lot of money as styles change very fast. To be able to keep up you need to keep buying new items just to keep on trend. This isn't very good for people who are on a budget and it can cause them to get into debt.

Money isn't the only problem though. The fashion industry can make people feel bad about themselves and feel bad about their body image. The industry puts out pictures of perfect models wearing amazing styles and people can feel pretty inadequate at the sight of them. If you don't feel so good about yourself to start with, this can be a big problem.

Checklist for success

- Think about how Caitlin Moran has used the varied structure and sentences to communicate her viewpoint.
- Think about the effect of each choice.
- Use at least one of these techniques in each paragraph of your rewrite.
- Evaluate your rewritten extract against the student example by reading aloud to check how the tone has become more engaging.

Applying the skills to plan and write an article for Paper 2 Question 5

You are learning to:
- understand how the examination question works
- think about the mark scheme skills in relation to your response
- plan for a point-of-view article
- consider a student response
- write up part of a response to the example examination task.

Testing: AO5 and AO6
For: Paper 2 Question 5

① Getting you thinking

a Look at this possible examination task for Paper 2 Question 5 and read the notes to help you understand what is expected of you.

> 'Keeping up with the latest fashions is a waste of time and of money; you do not need to be wealthy or have lots of free time to look cool.'
>
> Write an op-ed article for a broadsheet newspaper in which you explain your point of view on the statement.
>
> **(40 marks)**

You will be given a statement to work with. The statement will give you a topic and provide an opinion that you can either agree or disagree with.

You will then be given a format in which to write – perhaps an article, a letter or a speech. This format will be one that allows you to write in a more formal way to show your skills.

You will be asked to present your point of view by arguing, explaining or persuading your reader. You will need to think about who your audience actually is for the format you have been given.

You have 40 possible marks here – half of the marks for Paper 2. Twenty-four of the marks are for your content and organisation, 16 are for your spelling, punctuation, vocabulary, accurate grammar and sentence structures.

② Explore the skills

a Begin by asking yourself some basic questions. Make notes on your ideas.

- In the time that I have, how many different ideas should I plan? How will I organise my piece of work?
- What do I know about broadsheet news articles? What are their conventions?
- What type of language should I be using? What kind of language features should I be using?
- What techniques can I use to explain?
- Who would be reading this article? Who is my audience?

b Look at this extract from the Question 5 mark scheme.

- Why are the answers to the questions in Activity 2 important?
- What do you notice about the words that have been highlighted for you in the mark scheme?
- What key things do you need to do in your article to reach Level 3 of the mark scheme?

Lower Level 3 Clear **13–15 marks**	**Content** • Register is generally matched to audience • Generally matched to purpose • Vocabulary clearly chosen for effect and appropriate use of linguistic devices **Organisation** • Usually effective use of structural features • Writing is engaging with a range of connected ideas • Usually coherent paragraphs with a range of discourse markers

c Now look at the statement below. Do you agree with it or disagree? Do you have a more balanced view?

Write out the statement and annotate it with your ideas. Aim to gather five initial ideas.

'Keeping up with the latest fashions is a waste of time and of money; you do not need to be wealthy or have lots of free time to look cool.'

Fashions change quickly but classic styles always look good and don't date.

Lots of cool looks come from vintage shops.

d Now move on to organise your ideas into a paragraph plan and add topic sentences. You could use a grid like the one below or any of the planning methods from Week 23.

Ideas for explanation/Reasons for viewpoint	Topic sentence
Para 1:	.
Para 2:	
Para 3:	
Para 4:	
Para 5:	

a Read the following response to this task you are working on. As you read:

- make some notes on what the student has done well
- identify and note down what they might need to do in order to make more progress.

I think this is true because I don't have loads of money but I think I'm quite trendy and wear quite cool things. This is because I am dead careful about what I buy and this means that I don't just follow what my mates do and just buy anything that celebs wear.

I think that you can shop around and find great deals if you're clever. Like last weekend there were these big sales on but I ignored the obvious things right near the front of the shop and went and looked at the back. There are always these rails with odd sale items on which you can get if you know where to look. My friends think I'm mad but who is the mad one when they've paid loads and I've paid nothing?

Another thing is that you can go to charity shops and you can find great bargains there. Ok, loads of the stuff was left by older people but there is the odd gem if you look hard enough. I found this Gap dress that was like three pounds! I wore it to the school prom and no one knew where I'd got it. I just said it was in this sale and all my mates believed me.

The other thing is boot sales or jumble sales. My mum and dad love them and have their own stall so they're always dragging me along at the crack of dawn. The bad side is that I have to get up so early but on the good side we get to the field before most ordinary people. It means I can have a sneak look at what's on offer. Last month I bought an iPhone charger, which costs lots on the web if you want a proper one. I also saw these posters which were going cheap which were great for my art project.

So it is basically completely not the case that you need to be rich to be fashionable. There is no way I would call my family rich, my dad is a taxi-driver and my mum is a lunch-time dinner lady at my brother's school. You do need time to hunt stuff out, I give you that, but it's actually quite fun and I just think when I see my mates spending loads, who's the idiot now?

Anyway, I would definitely recommend charity shops, jumble sales and things like that if you want a bargain. You just need to know where to look I think.

Now read this comment from an examiner. How does this comment match with your own findings on the response?

Examiner comment:

The point of view expressed is reasonably clear, but ideas are somewhat jumbled and there is no real progression in the argument, suggesting the paragraphing and topic sentencing could have been more organised. The tone is also sometimes inappropriate with too much informality, especially in vocabulary choices. There is some attempt to use rhetorical devices, and to draw on anecdotal evidence for effect, but the language is not as fluent as it could be.

④ Final task

Go on to write up the first three paragraphs of your response to the examination task aiming to include some of the interesting rhetorical language features you learned about in Week 18 and the structural features you learned about in Week 24, Lesson 1.

Checklist for success

A successful response should include:

- a clear sense of your point of view and your reasons for it
- a convincing argument, supported by well-developed ideas
- language style and rhetorical features matched to the task and audience
- a structure that is persuasive and logical.

Applying the skills to plan and write a formal letter for Paper 2 Question 5

You are learning to:
- work step by step through an examination question
- plan for a letter expressing a point of view in response to a newspaper article
- practise using your knowledge of form and structure
- complete a written response to Paper 2 Question 5
- consider a student response and examiner comments
- evaluate your own response.

Testing: AO5 and AO6
For: Paper 2 Question 5

① Getting you thinking

Sometimes in the exam, rather than write an article or a speech, you may be asked to write a formal letter. This could be to an MP about an issue; to a college principal or a headteacher; or to the editor of a newspaper in response to an article that has been published. Your approach to the task will be just the same as for planning and writing a speech or article.

a Read this extract from an article, which takes a strong view about an unusual theme park.

In Dismaland, Banksy has created something truly depressing

This place is unreal. A dilapidated pub, desperate-looking big wheel and grim promenade perfectly express the melancholy of the British seaside. But that's just Weston-super-Mare on a cloudy morning. Dismaland is even stranger. Or so I hope, as I join the very first visitors to Banksy's "Bemusement Park" waiting to see what lies behind a miserably gothic sign on the battered facade of a decaying lido. [...]

Greeters – or rather, sulkers – wear Mickey Mouse ears and T-shirts that say DISMAL. Instead of being forced to smile all day they have to grimace all day.

Some are so good at it they appear genuinely pissed off. It's infectious, for me at least.

As cameraphones snap everything in sight, the gloom of the British seaside at its most dilapidated and moribund wells up in me. Memories of amusement arcades in Rhyl. Banksy has created something truly depressing. There at the heart of Dismaland is the fairytale castle, ruinous and rancid. The lake around it has a fountain that is a police water cannon. But an empty feeling is starting to hollow me out. Where's the fun I was promised? Well, I wasn't promised any fun, just dismalness. But surely not this dismal.

Perhaps you need intoxicants to enjoy Dismaland, and I was there at 11 in the morning. But its failure to create joy is self-defeating. […] Dismaland does not offer the energy and danger that real theme parks do. Instead, it brings together a lot of bad art by the seaside.

Jonathan Jones, *The Guardian*, 21 August 2015

b Now look at the following examination task.

A national newspaper has been covering the story of the theme park Dismaland and has stated:

'There is nothing more boring than visiting a place designed to make you enjoy yourself.'

Write a letter to the editor of the newspaper arguing your point of view on this statement.

② Explore the skills

You are going to work step by step through the examination task.

a Write out and collect ideas around the statement:

'There is nothing more boring than visiting a place designed to make you enjoy yourself.'

Do you agree or disagree? Annotate your statement with up to five ideas.

b Now move on to create your paragraph plan and topic sentences as you did in Week 24 Lesson 2.

Allow yourself 5–10 minutes for this process.

c Look at each of your topic sentences. How will you link them together? Which discourse markers could you use?

③ Develop the skills

Now think about your opening. Any letter to a newspaper begins with:

Dear Editor,

a Write up your opening paragraph. How will you engage the editor on the newspaper immediately?

b Write up paragraphs 2–4 on your plan, spending five minutes on each one. In each paragraph, think about keeping a balance of formal and informal language to keep your reader onside.

Aim to include some interesting structural features such as:

- very short sentences
- rhetorical questions
- hyperbolic questions
- personal anecdotes
- dashes to emphasise a particular idea (or ideas) to add variety and interest.

c Think about the final message you want to leave the newspaper editor with. Is there a 'call to action' in this case, or a strong reinforcement of your view?

Sign off your letter with:

Yours faithfully

> **Think back**
>
> Think back to the work that you did in Week 24.

Exam tip

Read over each paragraph before beginning the next one to check your work makes sense, and to check your spelling and punctuation. This is far more efficient than reading it over at the very end of an exam task when you are tired.

④ Final task

Read the following student response to the examination task and the annotations from the examiner. Ask yourself if your answer is:

- stronger than
- weaker than
- similar to

this response, which meets all of the skills descriptors for Level 3 of the mark scheme.

Dear Editor,

I recently read an article in your newspaper saying there is nothing more boring than visiting a place designed to make you enjoy yourself. I felt so strongly about that I had to respond. I've never heard something so wrong in all my life.

— uses an interesting structural feature and states opinion clearly

Having been to my fair share of theme parks and the like in my time I can tell you that with the right friends there can be nothing more fun. Some of my best memories are of the times that several people and I have spent an afternoon running from one attraction to another at a museum, castle or funfair.

— includes a brief anecdote and a list of three

But, strongly opinionated writer, I hear you cry, what about if you have to go on your own or with people with who you lack that oh so special bond of friendship? To this I reply, that this could ruin any trip. Apart from a few people who prefer their own company to that of others, any situation is made worse by the lack of friends and therefore improved by the presence of them. A situation that these places are very much designed for. That's why there's always more than one seat per row on a rollercoaster.

— matches register to audience and includes the reader

— adds interesting point to the argument

What an absurd notion it is that we would begin to dislike the very places that attempt to create the fundamental feeling of joy in us. Smiling is infectious and I often find that so is frowning. This I believe is the reason for this point of view: people passing on their negativity to others. So it is that I believe that it is up to us who still have our laugh and smile to pass them on to all those around us.

— vocabulary is becoming more sophisticated

— another clear idea to add to the argument. Paragraphs are structured well

There are many kinds of joy and therefore many different places to go to create it. Sure some won't work for some people. This is understandable, our difference and diversity as a species is what makes it so easy for us to advance and join together with our different opinions. A joke for one person might be a terrible insult for another. The easiest solution is to always try and see the best in a person or situation. A long line for one person could be a chore for one person but you could take the time to talk with others or play a game, catch up on some music or reading. The possibilities are endless.

If we can make mundane tasks fun then imagine what we could do to things that are already fun. Don't bring down the mood for the sake of it. Things are only boring if we let them be.

— a direct reference to audience, linked to task

Yours faithfully

Introducing comparative skills: viewpoint and perspective

You are learning to:
- develop your comprehension skills
- understand the importance of writers' viewpoints in this question
- work through two texts collating the writers' viewpoints with supporting evidence and inferences
- plan and write up the first part of an examination-style response.

Testing: AO3
For: Paper 2 Question 4

① Getting you thinking

The first step to being able to compare texts is to use your comprehension skills to identify the key ideas that each text has in common. You can support those ideas and make inferences to show your understanding. This first step uses exactly the same method as you used for Paper 2 Question 2: your AO1 skills. However, in this paper the focus is on the **writers' viewpoints and perspectives**. The ideas that you identify need to be those of each writer, not just about the content or topic of the text.

a Read the extract from an article about 'The Hole in the Wall', a project designed to study the educational ability of children living in poverty. Think about the following questions as you read:

- What does the **writer** do to test the slum children's learning?
- What is the main point the **writer** is making about learning?

Make notes in response to the following questions.

- Does he think the children want to learn?
- Does he think they find learning easy?
- Does he think their poverty is preventing them from learning?

In early 1999, some colleagues and I sunk a computer into the opening of a wall near our office in Kalkaji, New Delhi. The area was located in an expansive slum, with desperately poor people struggling to survive. The screen was visible from the street, and the PC was available to anyone who passed by.

The computer had online access and a number of programs that could be used, but no instructions were given for its use.

What happened next astonished us. Children came running out of the nearest slum and glued themselves to the computer. They couldn't get enough. They began to click and explore. They began to learn how to use this strange thing. A few hours later, a visibly surprised Vivek said the children were actually surfing the Web.

We left the PC where it was, available to everyone on the street, and within six months the children of the neighbourhood had learned all the mouse operations, could open and close programs, and were going online to download games, music and videos. We asked them how they had learned all of these sophisticated manoeuvres, and each time they told us they had taught themselves.

[...] The children seemed to learn to use the computer without any assistance. Language did not matter, and neither did education [...] Each time, the children were able to develop deep learning by teaching themselves.

Sugata Mitra, from www.edutopia.org/blog/self-organized-learning-sugata-mitra

② Explore the skills

a Still thinking about the article, complete the table and then make notes about:

- the **writer's viewpoint** on the subject
- the inferences you can draw from these statements and quotations.

Statement	Quotation	Inference
The writer tells us that they deliberately chose a very deprived area.	'desperately poor people struggling to survive'	It seems this was done on purpose to create an opportunity for very poor children to learn.
The writer observes that the children were interested in the computer.		
His view is that the children learned how to use it very quickly.		

b Now read the article below, written by Charles Dickens
more than 100 years before the first article.

The close, low chamber at the back, in which the boys were crowded, was so foul and
stifling as to be, at first, almost insupportable. But its moral aspect was so far worse
than its physical, that this was soon forgotten. Huddled together on a bench about the
room, and shown out by some flaring candles stuck against the walls, were a crowd of
boys, varying from mere infants to young men; sellers of fruit, herbs, lucifer-matches,
flints; sleepers under the dry arches of bridges; young thieves and beggars – with
nothing natural to youth about them: with nothing frank, ingenuous, or pleasant in
their faces; low-browed, vicious, cunning, wicked; abandoned of all help but this;
speeding downward to destruction; and UNUTTERABLY IGNORANT.
[…]

This was the Class I saw at the Ragged School. They could not be trusted with books;
they could only be instructed orally; they were difficult of reduction to anything like
attention, obedience, or decent behaviour; their benighted ignorance in reference to the
Deity, or to any social duty (how could they guess at any social duty, being so discarded
by all social teachers but the gaoler and the hangman!) was terrible to see. Yet, even
here, and among these, something had been done already. The Ragged School was of
recent date and very poor; but he had inculcated some association with the name of the
Almighty, which was not an oath, and had taught them to look forward in a hymn (they
sang it) to another life, which would correct the miseries and woes of this.

Charles Dickens, 'A Sleep to Startle Us', *Household Words*, 13 March 1852

c Look at the following statements. Find a piece of evidence
to support each one.

- In the first paragraph, Dickens thinks that the
  conditions and behaviour in the school are terrible.
- Dickens seems to think that the children in the school
  had some difficulty with learning.
- He feels there is hope for the children, however.

d This article is also about learning and education in deprived circumstances. Make some notes on the same questions as before.

- Do the children want to learn?
- Do they find learning easy?
- Does their poverty prevent them from learning?

Find evidence to support your answers.

③ Develop the skills

a What connects this article with the one before? Finish these sentences.

- **Both** articles are about…
- **Both** writers feel…
- **Both** writers think that…

b What are the differences between the two articles? Using **however** and **whereas**, finish these sentences.

- The first article presents the view that children can learn easily, **whereas** the second article…
- **However**, the tone of the first article seems very positive and optimistic, **whereas** the second article…
- **However**, the first article works through the story chronologically, **whereas** the second article…

④ Final task

Now pull your findings and evidence together. Write a plan to answer part of an examination-style task below.

Compare how the writers have conveyed their different views and perspectives on education for people living in deprived circumstances.

In your answer, you could:
- compare the different views and perspectives
- support your ideas with quotations from both texts.

What points will you include?

What evidence will you select?

What similarities and differences can you present?

Checklist for success

- Understand and explain the key connections between the two texts.
- Use the S.Q.I. structure (Statement, Quotation, Inference).
- Use the **both/however/whereas** key words to structure your comparison.

Developing comparative skills

You are learning to:
- practise your comprehension skills, thinking about the writers' viewpoints in both texts
- think about the writers' methods in presenting those viewpoints
- plan and write up the first part of an examination-style response.

Testing: AO3
For: Paper 2 Question 4

① Getting you thinking

In order to show higher order skills of comparison and move further up the mark scheme ladder, you will also need to show that you can compare the language and structure of the two texts – in other words, the different **methods** that each writer uses.

a Read the extract below, which is an editorial article from a broadsheet newspaper about boxing. Look closely at the quotations that have been highlighted for you.

> **Think back**
>
> This is exactly the same as you did for Paper 2 Question 3 in weeks 18 and 19 but this time, drawing ideas from both texts using your AO3 skills.

Source 1

Few would doubt Muhammad Ali's place as one of the great figures of the last century. He achieved global fame as an athlete, became a powerful spokesman for his people and a principled advocate for social justice – even forfeiting his champion's title rather than serve in Vietnam. But perhaps his greatest achievement is not yet complete. The eloquent testimony of his own deterioration into disability may yet prove his lasting legacy. For Muhammad Ali, once boxing's shining exponent, is now a living warning of the dangers of the ring. He has been reduced to virtual immobility, his once-fast tongue slowed and slurred – all because he took punches for three decades.

We mention him now because of the fate of a less-starred fellow boxer. On Saturday night Paul Ingle sustained serious brain injuries after losing to South Africa's Mbulelo Botile in Sheffield. He spent yesterday in hospital, in a "critical but stable" condition after surgeons laboured for two and half hours to remove a blood clot from his brain. Predictably, the British Boxing Board of Control has put on its concerned face, promising "to launch an inquiry" and look for "lessons to be learned".

But these cliches are no longer good enough. Boxing cannot sincerely "inquire" into the circumstances of Saturday's fight or look for lessons, as if what happened to Paul Ingle was a freak accident - like a plane collision or a rail crash. When a disaster of that kind strikes, it is because something wholly unexpected has happened. But for a man to suffer brain damage after his brain has been pummelled – deliberately and with precision – is wholly to be expected. It is no surprise at all. Ask Michael Watson, still confined to a wheelchair after his fight against Chris Eubank in 1991. Ask Gerald McClellan, beaten into a coma in 1995 and now in need of 24-hour-a-day care. Ask the family of Bradley Stone, killed by his 1994 bantamweight bout. Or take one last look at Muhammad Ali.

No liberal calls for a ban on any activity lightly. But we repeat our long-held belief that boxing has no place in a civilised society. To those who say a ban would only drive the sport underground, we point to bear-baiting and cock-fighting: they were banned and have all but vanished from British life. We wish the same fate for the sport which has laid waste to too many young men, including the greatest among them.

Leader, 'Ban this barbaric sport', from *The Guardian*, 18 December 2000

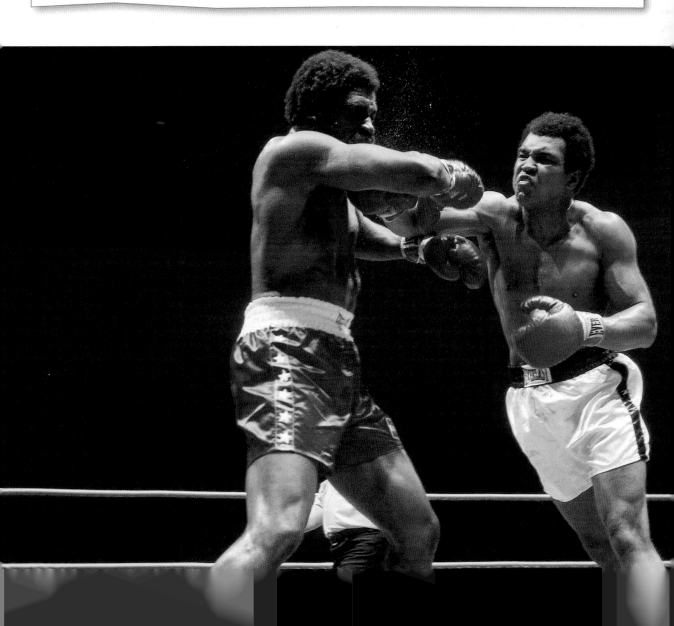

② Explore the skills

a Write three **statement** sentences, using any of the highlighted **quotations** to support your ideas and adding **inferences** to show your understanding in response to the following question.

> **What do you learn about the writer's viewpoint on boxing from those quotations?**

An example has been done to get you started:

> The writer disapproves of the sport of boxing. We can see this when he uses the example of boxing's greatest champion, Muhammad Ali as being, 'reduced to virtual immobility' because of the sport. This implies that the sport is dangerous and can lead to permanent damage.

③ Explore the skills

In order to answer this question fully, you need to think about what the writer has actually **done** to show you this viewpoint. In other words:

- what language features have they used?
- what structural features have they used?

These are the **methods** the writer has used to present their viewpoint effectively just as you learned to use different features in your own writing for Paper 2 Question 5.

a Look at the example below:

> The writer uses the verb 'reduced' to show how the former champion has been diminished and has lost his abilities. He uses other verbs such as 'slowed and slurred' to describe his speech. Added together with the noun phrase 'virtual immobility' this creates a picture of a broken man which backs up the writer's point of view about the sport.

— subject terminology

— examples

— comment on what it makes you think of, feel or imagine

— links to viewpoint

b Look back at your three S.Q.I. constructs. From the quotations, identify one aspect of language to 'zoom in on'. Write up your findings just as in the example above.

- Identify the language feature.
- Give an example of it.
- Make a comment on what it makes you think of, feel or imagine.

c Now read Source 2, which is an essay on boxing by William Hazlitt written in 1822. Again, as you read, think about what you are learning about this writer's viewpoint on boxing. Look closely at the highlighted quotations.

Source 2

In the first round every one thought it was all over. After making play a short time, the Gas-man flew at his adversary like a tiger, struck five blows in as many seconds, three first, and then following him as he staggered back, two more, right and left, and down he fell, a mighty ruin. There was a shout, and I said, "There is no standing this." Neate seemed like a lifeless lump of flesh and bone, round which the Gas-man's blows played with the rapidity of electricity or lighting, and you imagined he would only be lifted up to be knocked down again. [...]

If there had been a minute or more allowed between each round, it would have been intelligible how they should by degrees recover strength and resolution; but to see two men smashed to the ground, smeared with gore, stunned, senseless, the breath beaten out of their bodies; and then, before you recover from the shock, to see them rise up with new strength and courage, stand steady to inflict or receive mortal offence, and rush upon each other, "like two clouds over the Caspian" – this is the most astonishing thing of all: – this is the high and heroic state of man! [...]

Ye who despise the FANCY, do something to show as much pluck, or as much self-possession as this, before you assume a superiority which you have never given a single proof of by any one action in the whole course of your lives! – When the Gasman came to himself, the first words he uttered were, "Where am I? What is the matter!" "Nothing is the matter, Tom – you have lost the battle, but you are the bravest man alive."

William Hazlitt, from 'The Fight'

(d) Look at this student's planning method.

> Statement: This writer seems to admire boxing and boxer's skill.
>
> Supporting quotation: 'the Gas-man flew at his adversary like a tiger'
>
> Inference: suggests he sees the boxer as a fearless animal
>
> What the writer uses: simile
>
> Example: 'like a tiger'
>
> Effect: imagine a wild beast, no compassion, in for the kill

Using this planning method, collect two more ideas from the text to show what you learn about the writer's viewpoint on boxing.

(e) Go on to consider what language or structural feature the writer uses to present those ideas (the **method**). Include an example of this and a note on the effect.

(4) Final task

Using your planned ideas, write a clear opening paragraph in response to the task below.

Compare how the writers have conveyed their different views and perspectives on boxing.

In your answer, you should:

- compare the different views and perspectives
- compare the methods the writers use to convey their views and perspectives
- support your ideas with quotations from both texts.

Checklist for success

- Use the AO1 S.Q.I structure (Statement, Quotation, Inference).
- Lead into an AO2 point (writer's method + example + effect).
- Use the **both/however/whereas** key words to structure your comparison.

Applying comparative skills to Paper 2 Question 4

You are learning to:
- understand how the examination question works
- work step by step through an examination question, understanding and practising the method
- develop your ability to plan your response
- write up a complete response in a structured way to hit all of the required skills.

Testing: AO3
For: Paper 2 Question 4

---

① Getting you thinking

a Look closely at the format of the question for Paper 2 Question 4. Read the notes in the annotations to help you understand it more fully.

For this question, you need to refer to the whole of Source A together with the whole of Source B.

This does not mean you have to write about absolutely everything in both texts. It means you are free to select your ideas from anywhere in both texts.

Compare how the writers have conveyed their different views and perspectives of the behaviour of the authorities towards the poor.

The question is asking you about the views and experiences but look at the focus on 'how'.

You will be given a topic or aspect of the texts to focus on.

In your answer, you could:

- compare the different views and perspectives

This is asking you to identify what the viewpoints actually are – this is your S.Q.I. AO1 work.

- compare the methods they use to convey those different views and perspectives

This is asking you to think about the 'how' – in other words, what the writers are using. This is your AO2 skill.

- support your ideas with quotations from both texts.

Make sure you support your 'what' points with quotations and your 'how' points with examples.

(16 marks)

You have 16 marks here so just about 20 minutes to plan and write this response. A long essay is not expected in this time.

---

② Explore the skills

A student, when faced with the examination task above, began by using this thinking prompt:

When I think about the focus words, which parts of the text immediately seem to link to them? Choose my quotations.

a Read Source A and Source B, paying close attention to the quotations the student has chosen to highlight as a result of thinking about the **focus** of the task: 'the behaviour of the authorities towards the poor'

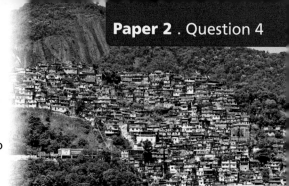

Source A: This broadsheet newspaper article looks at the issues of families losing their homes as Rio de Janeiro prepared to host the World Cup in 2014.

Rio World Cup demolitions leave favela families trapped in ghost town

From the roof of his home in the Favela do Metrô, Eomar Freitas enjoys one of the best views in town. Look south and you see the Christ the Redeemer statue towering over Rio's mountains. To the north stands the green and pink headquarters of Mangueira, the city's best-loved samba school.

5 And in between, one of the world's top sporting venues, the blue and grey Maracanã stadium, which will host the final of the 2014 football World Cup.

"We worked hard to build this place," said Freitas, 35 and unemployed, whose family moved to Rio from Brazil's impoverished north-east 20 years ago. They built a four-storey home where their wooden shack once stood. "It was a great place to live," he said.

10 Not any more. Since February, nearly all of the buildings surrounding Freitas's home have been levelled as part of work to revamp the city's infrastructure before the World Cup and the 2016 Olympic Games.

Redbrick shacks have been cracked open by earth-diggers. Streets are covered in a thick carpet of rubble, litter and twisted metal. By night, crack addicts squat in abandoned shacks, filling sitting
15 rooms with empty bottles, filthy mattresses and crack pipes improvised from plastic cups. The stench of human excrement hangs in the air.

"It looks like you are in Iraq or Libya," Freitas said, wading across mounds of debris that now encircle his home. "I don't have any neighbours left. It's a ghost town."

[...]

20 Among them are elderly women and children, including a four-year-old boy with microcephaly and cerebral palsy.

"We ask God to support us, so our hearts don't give out," said 77-year-old Sebastiana de Souza, who has spent 13 years in the favela, sharing a damp, cramped apartment with her daughter and four-year-old great-grandson who now plays football next to a heap of broken concrete,
25 abandoned furniture and discarded toys. Souza said she hoped to be relocated to a nearby estate. "It's sad. It used to be pretty around here."

The reasons for the favela's demolition are disputed. Locals believe authorities plan to replace it with a car park for the nearby stadium, a story endorsed by one demolition worker.

30 "The World Cup is on its way and they want this area," said Freitas. "I think it is inhumane."

Rio's housing secretary, Jorge Bittar, said the demolition was part of a £285m project to "transform" the region around the Maracanã, itself the centre of a £330m pre-World Cup revamp. Cultural centres, tree-lined plazas and a cinema would be built, he said.

"This is a very poor community, with very precarious homes [built] in an inappropriate area and
35 we are offering these families dignity," he said.

Tom Phillips, The *Guardian*, 26 April 2011

Source B: This extract comes from a report carried out into the forced removal of families from the Scottish Highlands in 1884.

Mr. Ross went from Glasgow to Greenyard all the way to investigate the case upon the spot, and found that Mr. Taylor, a native of Sutherland, well educated in the evicting schemes and murderous cruelty of that county, and Sheriff-substitute of Ross-shire, marched from Tain upon the morning of the 31st March, at the head of a strong party
5 of armed constables, with heavy bludgeons and firearms, conveyed in carts and other vehicles, allowing them as much ardent drink as they chose to take before leaving and on their march, so as to qualify them for the bloody work which they had to perform; fit for any outrage, fully equipped, and told by the sheriff to show no mercy to anyone who would oppose them, and not allow themselves to be called cowards, by allowing
10 these mountaineers victory over them. In this excited half-drunken state they came in contact with the unfortunate women of Greenyard, who were determined to prevent the officers from serving the summonses of removal upon them, and keep their holding of small farms where they and their forefathers lived and died for generations. But no time was allowed for parley; the sheriff gave the order to clear the way, and, be it said to his
15 everlasting disgrace, he struck the first blow at a woman, the mother of a large family, and large in the family way at the time, who tried to keep him back; then a general slaughter commenced; the women made noble resistance until the bravest of them got their arms broken, then they gave way. This did not allay the rage of the murderous brutes; they continued clubbing at the protectless creatures until every one of them was stretched on
20 the field, weltering in their blood, or with broken arms, ribs and bruised limbs. In this woeful condition many of them were hand-cuffed together, others tied with coarse ropes, huddled into carts, and carried prisoners to Tain.

Gilbert Beith, from *The Crofter Question*, 1884

Once they had highlighted the quotations, the student went on to think about these key questions and narrowed down their choices to select three ideas and quotations to work with.

> What ideas am I supporting with these quotations? Decide on my three supported statements.

> What inferences can I draw from those quotations?

b Think about the question plan for *your* three S.Q.I. constructs using a grid like the one below. An example has been done to get you started.

Statements	Supporting quotations	Inferences
Both of the texts deal with people losing their homes so the land can be used for other things.	'nearly all of the buildings …have been levelled'	Suggests people have been moved out with no concern for their land or property.
	'well educated in the evicting schemes and murderous cruelty'	Implies that in the past this was also done in a brutal way.

③ Develop the skills

Still planning, the student moved on to 'zoom in' on a key language or structural feature within their three chosen quotations and its effect.

> What aspects of language and/or structure has the writer used within those quotations?

> What effects are created by the language/structure choices made by the writer?

a Look closely at these quotations from the texts and the annotated extract from a student response below:

> nearly all of the buildings surrounding Freitas's home have been levelled as part of work to revamp the city's infrastructure before the World Cup and the 2016 Olympic Games.

> well educated in the evicting schemes and murderous cruelty of that county

Tom Phillips tells us very bluntly that people's homes have been ——————— statement

destroyed: 'all of the buildings surrounding Freitas's home have ——————— quotation to support

been levelled'. This suggests that no one's home was safe from ——————— inference

the bulldozers. The verb 'levelled' makes me think that whole ——————— language feature and example

areas were cleared with no regard for people and it seems very

brutal. ——————— effect

—————— comparison

In the same way Gilbert Beith suggests people were evicted in ——————— statement

a very brutal way and he has a poor opinion of the men who were

'well educated in the evicting schemes and murderous cruelty of ——————— quotation to support

that county.' This suggests that not only property but people ——————— inference

were harmed. The noun phrase 'murderous cruelty' makes me ——————— language feature and example

imagine criminal and brutal acts in the way both people and their ——————— effect

families were treated.

b Go on to note down a language or structural feature that you can see in each of your supporting quotations.

c Note down the possible effects by considering what it does to the text and what it makes you think of, feel or imagine.

④ Final task

You are now going to write up your complete answer to the examination task above. Use your planning notes and the following writing frame to help you structure all of the different elements of this 16-mark task. Aim to write up your response in no more than 15 minutes.

Intro:

Both of these articles deal with viewpoints about…

Para 1:

Tom Phillips feels that… (statement + quotation)

We see this through his use of… (method + example/comment)

whereas

Gilbert Beith feels that…

He uses…to show this.

Para 2:

Tom Phillips thinks about…

He shows this through his use of…

However

Beith thinks about…

He uses…to present this, creating the impression that…

Para 3:

In Source A, Phillips's point of view is one of…

presented through his use of…

Similarly,

Gilbert Beith's viewpoint is one of…

He presents this through the use of…, which…

Overall, both writers show similar views of…

Checklist for success

- Use the AO1 S.Q.I. structure (Statement, Quotation, Inference).

- Lead into an AO2 point (writer's method + example + effect).

- Use the **both/however/whereas** key words to structure your comparison.

Applying comparative skills to Paper 2 Question 4

You are learning to:
- understand how the mark scheme works
- work step by step through an examination question, understanding and practising the method
- develop your ability to plan your response
- write up a complete response in a structured way to hit all of the required skills
- evaluate your response against a student example.

Testing: AO3
For: Paper 2 Question 4

① Getting you thinking

a Look closely at this extract from the mark scheme for Paper 2 Question 4.

- What are the key differences between Levels 2 and 3?
- Looking at the 'ladder of skills', how does this ladder reflect the method you have worked on in Week 26?

Level 3 Clear, relevant 9–12 marks	• Compares ideas and perspectives in a clear and relevant way
	• Explains clearly how writers' methods are used
	• Selects relevant detail to support from both texts
	• Shows a clear understanding of the ideas and perspectives in both texts
Level 2 Some, attempts 5–8 marks	• Attempts to compare ideas and perspectives
	• Makes some comment on how writers' methods are used
	• Selects some appropriate detail, not always supporting, from one or both texts
	• Identifies some ideas and perspectives

② Explore the skills

You are now going to work through this examination task step by step to practise your skills.

For this question, you need to refer to the whole of Source A together with the whole of Source B.

Compare how the writers have conveyed their different views and perspectives of the way children and young people are treated in the articles.

In your answer, you could:

- compare the different views and perspectives
- compare the methods they use to convey those different views and perspectives
- support your ideas with quotations from both texts.

(16 marks)

(a) Begin by reading the two sources.

Source A is an autobiographical account of a young girl's experiences written in the 19th century.

My father was a glass blower. When I was eight years old my father died and our family had to go to the Bristol Workhouse. My brother was sent from Bristol workhouse in the same way as many other children were – cart-loads at a time. My mother did not know where he was for two years. He was taken off in the dead of night without her knowledge, and the parish officers would never tell her where he was.

It was the mother of Joseph Russell who first found out where the children were, and told my mother. We set off together, my mother and I, we walked the whole way from Bristol to Cressbrook Mill in Derbyshire. We were many days on the road.

Mrs. Newton fondled over my mother when we arrived. My mother had brought her a present of little glass ornaments. She got these ornaments from some of the workmen, thinking they would be a very nice present to carry to the mistress at Cressbrook, for her kindness to my brother. My brother told me that Mrs. Newton's fondling was all a blind; but I was so young and foolish, and so glad to see him again; that I did not heed what he said, and could not be persuaded to leave him. They would not let me stay unless I would take the shilling binding money. I took the shilling and I was very proud of it.

They took me into the counting house and showed me a piece of paper with a red sealed horse on which they told me to touch, and then to make a cross, which I did. This meant I had to stay at Cressbrook Mill till I was twenty one.

Sarah Ashton, interviewed in *The Ashton Chronicle*, 23 June 1849

Source 2 is a broadsheet newspaper article from 2011.

Britain's child soldiers

Denying those under the age of 18 the right to leave the army is outdated, immoral and in breach of UN guidelines

At 16 you are not old enough to vote, buy a pint in a pub or ride a motorbike. Yet you can join the armed forces, and commit yourself for four years beyond your 18th birthday. On becoming legally adult you can then be sent to the frontline in Afghanistan. A 16-year-old soldier can train with live ammunition, yet when he goes back to barracks in the evening he isn't old enough to rent an X-rated DVD of Apocalypse Now, a film dealing with the horrors of war – because it is too violent.

Notions of childhood change. During the siege of Mafeking in 1900, Robert Baden Powell recruited 12-year-old boys to deliver messages under fire. They wore khaki and their leader was the 13-year-old Warner Goodyear. But today Britain is the only European country to recruit into the regular army at 16. Perversely those young recruits are required to serve two years longer than those recruited at 18. Far from being a curious legal relic, this rule was re-introduced by the Labour government in 2008. After a six-month 'cooling-off' period there is no right to leave. While 'unhappy minors' may leave at the discretion of their commanding officer, the fact that there is no 'discharge as of right' leaves them uniquely open to bullying and that bullying is more serious if it happens because they cannot leave.

The situation of 16-year-old soldiers is sometimes compared to that of apprentices. Yet in what other 21st century apprenticeship can a breach of discipline lead to a court martial and time spent in military prison? In what other apprenticeship do you face such dangers? How many apprentice carpenters, brick layers or plumbers are found dead whether shot in the head or hanging from a beam? Yet that is what happened to four young recruits training at Deepcut barracks. A carpenter's skills are a guarantee of security in an economic downturn. There are more limited openings for trained marksmen. An infantryman returning from Helmand province has no guarantee of a job. David Cameron's call for a 'national change' in attitude towards mental health problems among former soldiers is highly welcome, but could his proposed 24-hour helpline be extended to soldiers who are currently serving or training in barracks?

While the UK no longer has conscription, those joining the army at 16 often come from the poorest and least educated backgrounds. For youngsters without other jobs to go to, a career in the army may be hard to resist. What other choices do they have? It is true that 16- and 17-year-olds are no longer deployed to conflict zones but decisions made as a child have irrevocable consequences as an adult. At the moment a young person making a decision at 16, with his parents' consent, has no right at the age of 18 to review that decision with an informed conscience.

Michael Bartlet, *The Guardian*, 11 March 2011

b Thinking about the focus of the question:

> **'different views and perspectives of the way children and young people are treated'**

plan your response by:

- selecting three quotations which show the way children and young people are treated from Source A
- writing three statements which focus on the writer's view of this from Source A
- repeating this process for Source B.

You could organise your ideas into a simple plan like the one below. Add in your inferences to the table.

	Source A	(whereas/however)	Source B
Statement:			
Supporting quotation:			
Inference:			

By doing this, you are dealing with the bottom two rungs of the mark scheme ladder: **the lower order skills**.

- Selects relevant detail to support from both texts
- Shows a clear understanding of the ideas and perspectives in both texts

③ Develop the skills

Now you are going to move on to think about the higher order skills: the ones that take you to the highest mark in the level. Plan to include those ideas in your response.

• Explains clearly how writers' methods are used

a Finish organising your ideas into your clear and methodical plan:

	Source A	(whereas/however)	Source B
Statement:			
Supporting quotation:			
Inference:			
What the writer uses:			
Example:			
Effect:			

④ Final task

a Read the student response below, together with the examiner comments.

Sarah Ashton tells us that children were treated very badly in the past as she tells us about her brother who was 'taken off in the dead of night' from the workhouse. The phrase 'dead of night' sounds very spooky and a scary experience for a child.

The newspaper article also talks about how children were treated badly in the past: 'Robert Baden Powell recruited 12 year old boys to deliver messages under fire.'

The children in Source A seem to be tricked into working. Sarah tells us she made a cross on a piece of paper and 'This meant I had to stay at Cressbrook Mill until I was twenty one.'

Source B also shows how young people in the army have to stay for a long time: 'young recruits are required to serve two years longer than those recruited at 18'

Both of the writers use facts here.

The writer of the second article tells us that it is better to be an apprentice than in the army, asking 'In what other apprenticeship do you face such dangers?' He uses a rhetorical question to make us think that being in the army so young is not a good choice.

However, in Sarah's interview her brother did not have any choice at all about being an apprentice in the mill and Sarah doesn't understand what she is signing up to do. This is like the writer in the second article who says that a young soldier today is not able to 'review that decision' to be in the army.

Examiner comment:

This answer identifies some of the key ideas in both texts but does not really pinpoint the writers' viewpoints of the two situations. They could, for example, have thought about whether each writer was happy with these situations or whether they were, in fact, critical of them. The answer uses some detail and quotations from both texts, which is helpful, and does support the ideas but again, does not always tells us a great deal about the writer's view. They identify the use of facts but do not link this finding into their response in any way by thinking what this adds to the source. The comment on the rhetorical question is more helpful but could be developed to include why the writer chooses this method more than once. However, this response does attempt to compare throughout and as such would be a reasonable Level 2 response. 7 marks.

> **Think back**
>
> Aim to keep all of your work **clear** and **relevant** using the planning method and writing frame you have worked with in Weeks 26 and 27.

b Thinking about the advice in the examiner comment, go on to write up your final response to the examination task in 15–20 minutes.

Checklist for success

- Understand and explain the key connections between the two texts.
- Use the AO1 S.Q.I. structure (Statement, Quotation, Inference).
- Lead into an AO2 point (writer's method + example + effect).
- Use the **both/however/whereas** key words to structure your comparison.

End-of-term progress assessment task: Walking through a mock Paper 2

You are aiming to show that

- you can read an unseen non-fiction text carefully and with understanding, picking out the right types of information
- you can read both modern and 19th century texts carefully and with understanding, picking out the right types of information
- you can support your ideas on those texts by being able to select quotations from both texts
- you can make inferences about what things might mean or suggest to you to show your understanding of both texts
- you can show knowledge about the choices of language and language features used in a given text and the effect those choices have on you, the reader.

Testing: AO1 and AO2
For: Paper 2 Questions 1, 2, 3

What you can expect in the exam

In Paper 2 Section A of the exam, you will be asked to read two pieces of source material from non-fiction texts. One will be from the 19th century and the other will be more modern, from either the 20th or 21st century. You are unlikely to have seen the passages before. Your job is to apply your skills of reading and analysis to the questions about the sources. You have one hour to read and complete four questions worth 40 marks – half of the marks on the paper.

Step 1

Begin by reading the extract below carefully. It is a broadsheet newspaper article about Queen Elizabeth II's Diamond Jubilee in 2015 celebrating the Queen's 60-year reign.

Source A

> ### The Queen's Diamond Jubilee: I have memories to treasure forever
>
> The Queen has described the public's ecstatic response to her **Diamond Jubilee** as "a humbling experience" as she thanked the nation at the climax of a spectacular weekend of celebration.
>
> In a rare televised address to Britain and the Commonwealth, the sovereign said
> 5 she would "treasure" the memories of the past week.
>
> For the third consecutive day, hundreds of thousands of people flooded into the capital to pay tribute to "Elizabeth the Great" as one banner described her.

The Queen was visibly moved as she stepped out onto the balcony of Buckingham Palace to see The Mall filled with people who had, once again, shrugged off cold
10 and rain to cheer her on.

"Oh my goodness, how extraordinary!" Her Majesty said as she saw the ocean of red, white and blue stretching as far as the eye could see.

Only six members of the Royal family appeared on the balcony, and as a statement of the endurance of the monarchy, it could not have been bolder.

15 Flanked by her heir, the Prince of Wales, and his eventual successor, the Duke of Cambridge, the Queen used the deliberately pared-down balcony appearance to tell the nation its future is in safe hands. By showing the world the future of the monarchy, starting with the Prince of Wales, she was also delivering a clear message that there is no question of the succession skipping a generation.

20 She described the throng serenading her in The Mall with the National Anthem as "marvellous" and "incredible". Her only regret was that the Duke of Edinburgh, recovering in hospital from a bladder infection, was not by her side. "She's missing him, obviously," the Earl of Wessex said after a brief hospital visit.

In her televised address, one of only a handful she has made outside her
25 traditional Christmas message, she said: "The events that I have attended to mark my Diamond Jubilee have been a humbling experience.

"It has touched me deeply to see so many thousands of families, neighbours and friends celebrating together in such a happy atmosphere."

30 She said she and the Duke of Edinburgh wanted to pass on their "special thanks" to the organisers of the events, which had been a "massive challenge".

She said: "I hope that memories of all this year's happy events will brighten our lives for many years to come. I will continue to treasure and draw inspiration
35 from the countless kindnesses shown to me in this country and throughout the Commonwealth. Thank you all."

[…]

On a day when the fun of the previous three days gave way to more formal celebrations, the Queen decided that those in the direct line of succession should take centre stage.

40 The Prince of Wales and Duchess of Cornwall, the Duke and Duchess of Cambridge and Prince Harry were the only members of the Royal family who walked with her down the aisle for a Service of Thanksgiving, lunched with her at Westminster Hall and drove through London in open carriages before their 11-minute balcony appearance.

45 Aides said the Queen wanted the nation, and the watching world, to concentrate on the future of the monarchy, and it was a message that was received loud and clear.

[…]

The day began with the service at St Paul's Cathedral, attended by a congregation of 2,000 invited guests including more than 50 members of the Royal family.

50 […]

Then came the moment those lining the streets had been waiting for since the early morning, or even overnight – the carriage procession, accompanied by more than 100 guardsmen on horseback in full dress uniform.

[…]

55 After driving down Whitehall and rounding the corner of Trafalgar Square, the procession entered The Mall, lined by hundreds of guardsmen in bearskins and red tunics, and crowds standing 10 to 20 deep.

[…]

Then, at 3.25pm, the doors behind the balcony opened and the Queen made her
60 appearance, beaming and waving at the masses below.

[…]

"It's a marvellous time," the Queen said as she waved again to the crowd after the National Anthem. The Duke of Cambridge leaned to her and said "[listen to] to those cheers for you". Finally, as she turned to go back inside, she added: "Incredible people.
65 Bless them."

Gordon Rayner, *The Telegraph*, 5 June 2012

Step 2

Now read your first examination task and write out your responses carefully. This is testing your basic skills for AO1.

Question 1

Look again at the section highlighted in green.

Choose four statements below that are TRUE.

Choose a maximum of four statements. **(4 marks)**

a) The Queen thanked the nation at the beginning of the weekend.

b) Hundreds of people gathered to see the Queen.

c) The Queen was celebrating her diamond jubilee.

d) The Queen did not move as she stood on the balcony.

e) It is rare for the Queen to speak to the nation on television.

f) The Queen greeted well-wishers from the balcony of Buckingham Palace.

g) The Queen was looking out towards the ocean.

h) She appeared with six members of her family.

Step 3

When you are happy with your response, move on to the next task. This is also testing your skills for AO1.

Read this second piece of source material carefully. It is taken from the journal of Queen Victoria describing her own Diamond Jubilee celebrations in London in 1897.

Source B

A never to be forgotten day. No one ever I believe, has met with such an ovation as was given to me, passing through those 6 miles of streets, including Constitution Hill. The crowds were quite indescribable & their enthusiasm truly marvellous & deeply touching. The cheering was quite deafening, & every face seemed to be filled
5 with real joy. I was much moved & gratified...I started from the State Entrance in an open state landau, drawn by 8 creams, dear Alix, looking very pretty in lilac, & Lenchen, sitting opposite me. I felt a good deal agitated, & had been so all these days, for fear anything might be forgotten or go wrong. Bertie & George C. rode one on each side of the carriage, Arthur (who had charge of the whole military

10 arrangements) a little in the rear...Before leaving I touched an electric button, by
which I started a message which was telegraphed throughout the whole Empire.
It was the following: "From my heart I thank my beloved people, may God bless
them". At this time the sun burst out. Vicky was in the carriage nearest to me, not
being able to go in mine, as her rank as Empress prevented her sitting with her
15 back to the horses, for I had to sit alone. Her carriage was drawn up by 4 blacks,
richly caparisoned in red. We went up Constitution Hill & Piccadilly & there were
seats right along the former, where my own servants & personal attendants, &
members of the other Royal Households, the Chelsea Pensioners & the children of
the Duke of York's & Greenwich schools had seats. St James' Street was beautifully
20 decorated with festoons of flowers across the road, & many loyal inscriptions.
Trafalgar Square was very striking & outside the National Gallery stands were
erected for the House of Lords. The denseness of the crowds was immense, but
the order maintained wonderful. The streets in the Strand are now quite wide, but
one misses Temple Bar. Here, the Lord Mayor received me & presented the sword,
25 which I touched. He then immediately mounted his horse, in his robes & galloped
[sic] past bare headed carrying the sword, preceding my carriage accompanied by
his Sheriffs. As we neared St Paul's the Procession was often stopped, & the crowds
broke out into singing "God Save The Queen". In one house were assembled the
survivors of the Charge of Balaclava. In front of the Cathedral, the scene was most
30 impressive. All the Colonial troops, on foot, were drawn up round the Square. My
carriage, surrounded by all the Royal Princes was drawn up close to the steps,
where the Clergy were assembled, the Bishops, in rich copes, with their croziers, the
Arch Bishop of Canterbury & the Bishop of London, each holding a very fine one.
A Te Deum was sung, especially composed by Dr Martin, the Lord's Prayer, most
35 beautifully chanted, a special Jubilee prayer, & the benediction concluded the short
service, preceded by the singing of the old 100th, in which everyone joined. "God
Save The Queen" was also sung...

Royal Archives

British Monarchy website

http://www.queen-victorias-scrapbook.org/contents/8-1.htm

Question 2

You need to refer to Source A and Source B for this question:

The ways that Queen Victoria and Queen Elizabeth II celebrated their Diamond Jubilee were similar.

Use details from both sources to write a summary of the similarities. **(8 marks)**

Checklist for success

- Make clear statements in your own words, addressing the question directly.
- Support those statements with selected quotations.
- Make inferences to show your understanding.
- Remember this is an 8-mark short answer task.

Step 4

When you are happy with your response, move on to the next task. This is testing your skills for AO2.

Question 3

You now need to refer only to Source B, Queen Victoria's journal entry about her Jubilee celebration (the section highlighted in yellow).

How does Queen Victoria use language to convey her feelings about the Diamond Jubilee celebrations? **(12 marks)**

Checklist for success

- In this response, select no more than four language features.
- Make sure you give an example of each one.
- Make a comment that explains what the feature is actually doing.
- Develop that comment by deciding on what it makes you think of, feel or imagine.

End-of-term progress assessment task: Walking through a mock Paper 2

You are aiming to show that:
- you can read and compare both modern and 19th century texts carefully and with understanding
- you can support your ideas on both texts by being able to select quotations
- you can make inferences to show your understanding of both texts
- you can compare the choices of language or structural features used in both texts and the effect those choices have on you, the reader.

Testing: AO3
For: Paper 2 Question 4

In this second session, you are going to complete the final question of Section A of the paper, testing AO3 and representing 16 of the 40 marks. You will find it helpful to read both of the extracts from last time before you begin.

Question 4 will ask you to focus on both pieces of source material and select your ideas from anywhere in the sources.

Step 1

Carefully read your examination task for Question 4 and plan your answer using the bullet points to guide you. This is testing your skills for AO3.

> **Question 4**
>
> For this question, you need to refer to the whole of Source A together with the whole of Source B.
>
> **Compare how the writers have conveyed their different ideas and perspectives about the Diamond Jubilee celebrations.**
>
> In your answer, you could:
> - compare their perspectives on the Diamond Jubilee
> - compare the methods they use to present the ideas and perspectives
> - support your ideas with quotations from both texts.
>
> **(16 marks)**

Checklist for success

- Understand and explain the key connections between the two texts.
- Use the AO1 S.Q.I. structure (Statement, Quotation, Inference).
- Lead into an AO2 point (writer's method + example + effect).
- Use the **both/however/whereas** key words to structure your comparison.

End-of-term progress assessment task: Walking through a mock Paper 2

In this final session of your Paper 2 mock exam, you are going to complete Section B of the paper, testing AO5 and AO6 and representing 40 marks. There will be one task to respond to.

Remember:

- you are advised to spend 45 minutes on the exam task
- you must write in full sentences
- you are reminded of the need to plan your answer
- you should leave enough time to check your work at the end.

> **Some people think the Royal Family are an important part of British heritage and tradition; others feel they are a costly waste of taxpayers' money.**
>
> Write a speech for a debate in your college about whether the Royal Family should be a part of Britain's future or whether they should be abolished.
>
> **(24 marks for content and organisation**
> **16 marks for technical accuracy)**   **(40 marks)**

Checklist for success

A successful response should include:

- a clear sense of your point of view and your reasons for it
- a convincing argument, supported by well-developed ideas
- language style and rhetorical features matched to the task and audience
- a structure that is persuasive and logical.

You are aiming to show that:
- you can plan an examination task, testing point-of-view writing
- you can use paragraphing and topic sentences effectively
- you can apply your knowledge of structure and use interesting structural features appropriate to the given form
- you can apply your knowledge of language and use a range of vocabulary and language features appropriate to the register
- you can include some accurate complex spellings
- you can control the tense of your verbs and agreement
- you can punctuate your work in a way that shows you are clear and accurate
- you can vary your sentence structures for effect.

Testing: AO5 and AO6
For: Paper 2 Question 5

Check your progress: Section A

Grade 8

- I can summarise and critically evaluate with detailed and perceptive understanding.
- I can understand and respond with insight to explicit and implicit meanings and viewpoints.
- I can analyse and critically evaluate detailed aspects of language, grammar and structure.
- I can back up my understanding and opinions with judicious references and supporting quotations.
- I can make convincing links between texts.

Grade 5

- I can summarise and evaluate with accuracy and clear understanding.
- I can understand and make valid responses to explicit and implicit meanings and viewpoints.
- I can analyse and evaluate relevant aspects of language, grammar and structure.
- I can support my understanding and opinions with sensibly chosen references to texts.
- I can make sensible links between texts.

Grade 2

- I can describe and summarise with some accuracy and understanding.
- I can respond in a straightforward way to most explicit information and viewpoints.
- I can make some relevant comments about language and structure.
- I can support my comments and opinions with some general references.
- I can make straightforward links between texts.

Check your progress:
Section B

Grade 8

- I can communicate with impact.
- I can produce an ambitious and effectively structured piece of writing.
- I can use a wide range of well-selected sentence types and structures, and use precise vocabulary for impact.
- I can spell, punctuate and use grammar accurately so that writing is virtually error-free.

Grade 5

- I can communicate effectively and hold my reader's interest.
- I can produce a well-structured and purposeful piece of writing.
- I can vary my sentence types and structures, and use vocabulary for effect.
- I can spell, punctuate and use grammar accurately with occasional errors.

Grade 2

- I can communicate simply in English with some clarity for my reader.
- I can produce writing with a basic structure and some awareness of purpose.
- I can show some control over sentences and use familiar vocabulary.
- I can spell, punctuate and use grammar with a little accuracy.

Final mock examination: Paper 1

Read **Source A**: an extract from the novel *The Electric Michaelangelo* by Sarah Hall. In this extract a young boy, living in a seaside town, witnesses an extraordinary event.

Source A:

In March of 1917, sometime between the hours of ten and eleven at night, a faulty fuse sparked on the western pier, inside its most majestic building. The little smoulder gathered strength and in the strong sea breeze it spun into a persistent glut of flame. Then the fire, suddenly very confident, spread to the ground-floor ceiling of the structure and lay upside 5 down across its rafters. The great pavilion of the Taj Mahal went up in a blaze the likes of which the town had never seen before.

[...]

Cy pulled back the curtain of his window. He'd been reading when an undefined patch of light, out of keeping with the glare of the streetlamps on the promenade, caught his 10 eye. His mother at her window saw wings of orange curving up the sides of the main dome, mimicking its shape, tormenting it with the authority to destroy it. Both ran to the front door, knocking awake their guests. An opportunistic buzz quickly went through Morecambe.

[...]

15 The townsfolk and the first of the season's visitors made their way out of their houses and hotels and down to the beach, awed and hurriedly, as if late for the performance, though it looked in no danger of finishing before time.

[...]

Fire itself would have been incendiary beauty enough for one evening. But then, it snowed. 20 First it snowed lightly, a flake or two on the heads of the bemused onlookers, like winter waving a handkerchief from a distant carriage of the train, taking it away. Someone close to Cy in the crowd cheered, presuming the snow would extinguish the blaze, as if one tear could put out the fire of a tormented heart!

[...]

25 Cy found Morris Gibbs in the crowd, for his red hair seemed like a portion of the fire itself in the light, and he pulled on his arm. They walked closer to the blaze, so close Cy could feel his face change texture, crisping, broiling. [...] The snow blew fast to the right, arched upwards, fell was chaotic, then resumed its course. Cy looked up. Oh. The snow. The snow was on fire. How could that be? [...] And yet it was so. Fire and ice. There above him.

30 The brilliant snow moved like thousands of migrating flaming birds across the
sky, flocking, reforming, conflagrating. It was like meteors swarming and rushing
on some swift and undisclosed passage, riding the rapids of the cosmos. Or like
being spun with his eyes open in a circle on a clear night except that he was
standing still and the sky was whirling of its own accord. It was like pieces of a
35 mirror being smashed in the heavens, in a fury of narcissistic disappointment. He
was ten years old and dizzy with amazement.

   – Look at it. It's beautiful, Morris. It's beautiful.

   – It is at that.

And the two boys stood watching the impossibility of the entire western portion
40 of the sky alight with burning snowflakes.

Question 1

Read again the first part of the source highlighted in blue. List four things you learn from the extract about the fire. (4 marks)

> *Checklist for success*
>
> - Present your response to Question 1 in a numbered list.
> - Use short, sharp clear sentences.
> - Use only things that are given to you in the extract and that you can identify as being true.

Question 2

Look in detail at the section highlighted in yellow.

How does the writer use language here to describe what happened that evening?

You could include the writer's choice of:
- words and phrases
- language features and techniques
- sentence forms. (8 marks)

> *Checklist for success*
>
> - Select no more than three language ideas or special effects
> - Make sure you give an example of each one.
> - Make a comment that explains the effect of the example by deciding on what it makes you think of, feel or imagine.

Question 3

You now need to think about the whole of the source.

This text is an extract from a novel. How has the writer structured the text to interest you as a reader?

You could write about:

- what the writer focuses your attention on at the beginning
- how and why the writer changes the focus as the source develops
- any other structural features that interest you.   **(8 marks)**

Checklist for success

- Select no more than three structural ideas or special effects.
- Give an example of each one or indicate where they are with a line reference.
- Make a comment that explains what the feature does to the text and the effect this has on you, the reader.

Question 4

Focus your answer on the second part of the source from 'Fire itself would have been incendiary beauty enough for one evening.' (line 19) to the end.

A student, having read this section of the text, said: 'The writer creates a real sense of how the events affect Cy.' To what extent do you agree?

In your response, you could:

- consider your own impressions of how Cy is affected by the events
- evaluate how the writer creates a sense of the events and Cy's reactions
- support your opinions with quotations from the text.   **(20 marks)**

Checklist for success

- Show your AO1 skills in addressing the first bullet point by using your statement + quotation + inference method.
- Show your AO2 skills in addressing the 'how' bullet point by identifying and exemplifying aspects of language with comments on effect.
- Work with no more than three ideas.

Question 5

You are advised to spend 45 minutes on the exam task.

You must write in full sentences.

You are reminded of the need to plan your answer.

You should leave enough time to check your work at the end.

Select one of the tasks below.

Either:

Write a description suggested by this picture:

Checklist for success

- Write a structured five-point planning journey.
- Remember to use topic sentences.
- Plan a selection of interesting language and structural special effects to include in the description.

Or:

Write a short story in which two friends witness an exciting or unusual event.

(24 marks for content and organisation

16 marks for technical accuracy)   **(40 marks)**

Checklist for success

- Ensure your story has an effective opening, a complication, a climax and resolution.
- Ensure you have paragraphed each of these shifts clearly.
- Check back through your spelling and punctuation to ensure it makes your work clear, effective and varied.

Check your progress: Section A

Grade 8

- I can summarise and critically evaluate with detailed and perceptive understanding.
- I can understand and respond with insight to explicit and implicit meanings and viewpoints.
- I can analyse and critically evaluate detailed aspects of language, grammar and structure.
- I can back up my understanding and opinions with judicious references and supporting quotations.

Grade 5

- I can summarise and evaluate with accuracy and clear understanding.
- I can understand and make valid responses to explicit and implicit meanings and viewpoints.
- I can analyse and evaluate relevant aspects of language, grammar and structure.
- I can support my understanding and opinions with sensibly chosen references to texts.

Grade 2

- I can describe and summarise with some accuracy and understanding.
- I can respond in a straightforward way to most explicit information and viewpoints.
- I can make some relevant comments about language and structure.
- I can support my comments and opinions with some general references.

Check your progress: Section B

Grade 8

- I can communicate with impact.
- I can produce an ambitious and effectively structured piece of writing.
- I can use a wide range of well-selected sentence types and structures, and use precise vocabulary for impact.
- I can spell, punctuate and use grammar accurately so that writing is virtually error-free.

Grade 5

- I can communicate effectively and hold my reader's interest.
- I can produce a well-structured and purposeful piece of writing.
- I can vary my sentence types and structures, and use vocabulary for effect.
- I can spell, punctuate and use grammar accurately with occasional errors.

Grade 2

- I can communicate simply in English with some clarity for my reader.
- I can produce writing with a basic structure and some awareness of purpose.
- I can show some control over sentences and use familiar vocabulary.
- I can spell, punctuate and use grammar with a little accuracy.

Final mock examination: Paper 2

Paper 2 Mock Examination

Read **Source A:** a piece of journalism about young people voting in elections, from the American online newspaper *The Huffington Post*, published on 12 November 2015.

Source A:

My generation, Generation Y (aka The Millennials), often gets a bad name. We're lazy. We're self-involved. We take too many selfies and are too involved in celebrity news. We are too involved in technology. And I've about had it, like 60 percent of my peers.

But it seems that when election season rolls around, the lazy stereotype starts to show its
5   true colors.

According to data […] 21.3 percent — or around 10 million of us turned out to vote in the 2014 midterm elections. The Center for American Progress found that in the 2012 election our generation had 64 million eligible voters, yet only 26 percent of us actually voted. That means a large number of us, 74 percent, didn't vote.

10 So what's holding us back from going to the polls? Is it really our laziness? Is it the candidates? Maybe they are talking about issues we don't care about or don't know enough about. Are they not using resources to reach us in the correct way?

Contrary to popular belief, we don't really hate politicians or politics. With the age of the Internet, we should be more informed than any generation that has come before us.
15 Everything is at our fingertips. There are videos, websites, social media accounts, anything, you name it, that tells us all about the topics and candidates.

[…]

We are one of the biggest segments of the population and we are just on the cusp (or already in) adulthood. But many young people think that their vote doesn't count and
20 politics isn't relevant in their lives.

Twenty-two-year-old Mary Anna Billingsley believes that, as a generation, we fail to acknowledge how much politics is really involved in our lives. She told me:

'They fail to realize that we have taxes taken out of our income, we have laws that we must follow or we face consequences, we have liberties that we take for granted, we have a right
25 *to vote for the individuals we think will best govern… It's preposterous for anyone to say that politics isn't relevant in their lives because they truly do have a place in nearly every aspect of our lives. My parents always say that if you don't vote in an election, you can't complain about the individual or their opponent when one is elected because you did not use your right to vote, and thus, lost your right to complain.'*

30 […]

Yes, voting is a right in our country, but it is also a great privilege that a lot of people have to fight — and even die — for. The democratic process does not work if we are not connected and doing something.

Geenah Krisht, 22, believes that people who do not vote are lazy and/or ignorant:

35 *'There are countries in this world in which voting is not a citizen's right. And, there are people in our country that are fighting to become voting citizens. You only have one life, and if you're privileged enough to be born a citizen of the United States, you should let your voice be heard.... No matter who is listening or who you think is listening, exercise your right to vote.'*

40 [...]

We actually do care about issues like abortion and immigration, and we also care a lot about the economy and jobs, climate change and what's happening in other countries. It's because we were told growing up that we could be anything we wanted to be, that includes changing the world. We have become more aware of human rights violations in other 45 countries. We are activists, and we would like our government to reflect the world we want to see.

I'm invoking one of our stereotypes right now: Hey Washington, pay attention to us. We are the ones you should be targeting because — here's a scary thought — we are the future. But, in order to invoke the change we want to see, we have to speak up. And for our 50 country's sake, the 74 percent of you who didn't vote in the last presidential election — go vote.

Hanan Esaili, *The Huffington Post,* 12 November 2015

Question 1

Look again at this section.

My generation, Generation Y (aka The Millennials), often gets a bad name. We're lazy. We're self-involved. We take too many selfi es and are too involved in celebrity news. We are too involved in technology. And I've about had it, like 60 percent of my peers.

But it seems that when election season rolls around, the lazy stereotype starts to show its true colors.

According to data [...] 21.3 percent — or around 10 million of us turned out to vote in the 2014 midterm elections. The Center for American Progress found that in the 2012 election our generation had 64 million eligible voters, yet only 26 percent of us actually voted. That means a large number of us, 74 percent, didn't vote.

Choose four statements below that are TRUE.

Choose a maximum of four statements. (4 marks)

a) Generation Y is generally very well thought of.

b) Around 10 million young Americans turned out to vote in the 2014 midterm elections.

c) Young Americans can be portrayed as lazy and self-involved.

d) 74% of young Americans turned out to vote in 2012.

e) Young people don't take enough selfies.

f) During elections, young people seem to be lazy about voting.

g) 64 million young people could have voted in 2012.

h) 60% of the writer's peers are involved in technology.

Now read **Source B:** a piece of autobiographical writing by Emmeline Pankhurst who led the campaign for British women to have the right to vote. In it, she describes a time when campaigners attempted to take a petition to the Houses of Parliament.

Source B:

How to tell the story of that dreadful day, Black Friday, as it lives in our memory – how to describe what happened to English women at the behest of the English government, is a difficult task. [...] The plain facts, baldly stated, I am aware will strain credulity.

Remember that the country was on the eve of a general election, and that the Liberal Party
5 needed the help of Liberal women. [...] What the government feared, was that Liberal women would be stirred by our sufferings into refraining from doing election work for the party. So the government conceived a plan whereby the Suffragettes were to be punished, were to be turned back and defeated in their purpose of reaching the House, but would not be arrested. Orders were evidently given that the police were to be present in the streets,
10 and that the women were to be thrown from one uniformed or ununiformed policeman to another, that they were to be so rudely treated that sheer terror would cause them to turn back. I say orders were given and as one proof of this I can first point out that on all previous occasions the police had first tried to turn back the deputations and when the women persisted in going forward, had arrested them. At times individual policemen had
15 behaved with cruelty and malice towards us, but never anything like the unanimous and wholesale brutality that was shown on Black Friday.

[...]

At intervals of two or three minutes small groups of women appeared in the square, trying to join us at the Strangers' Entrance. They carried little banners inscribed with various
20 mottoes. [...] These banners the police seized and tore in pieces. Then they laid hands on the women and literally threw them from one man to another. Some of the police used their fists, striking the women in their faces, their breasts, their shoulders.

One woman I saw thrown down with violence three or four times in rapid succession until at last she lay only half conscious against the curb, and in a serious condition was carried away
25 by kindly strangers. Every moment the struggle grew fiercer, as more and more women arrived on the scene. Women, many of them eminent in art, in medicine and science, women of European reputation, subjected to treatment that would not have been meted out to criminals, and all for the offence of insisting upon the right of peaceful petition.

The struggle lasted for about an hour, more and more women successfully pushing their
30 way past the police and gaining the steps of the House. Then the mounted police were summoned to turn the women back. But, desperately determined, the women, fearing not the hoofs of the horses or the crushing violence of the police, did not swerve from their purpose. [...] For a long time, nearly five hours, the police continued to hustle and beat the women, the crowds becoming more turbulent in their defence. Then, at last the police were
35 obliged to make arrests. One hundred and fifteen women and four men, most of them bruised and choked and otherwise injured, were arrested.

Emmeline Pankhurst, from *My Own Story*

Question 2

You need to refer to Source A and Source B for this question:

The ways that people feel strongly about the importance of voting in both sources is similar.

Use details from both sources to write a summary of the similarities. **(8 marks)**

> **Checklist for success**
> - Make clear statements in your own words, addressing the question directly.
> - Support those statements with selected quotations.
> - Make inferences to show your understanding.
> - Remember this is an 8-mark short answer task.

Question 3

You now need to refer only to this section of Source B, Emmeline Pankhurst's autobiographical work.

At intervals of two or three minutes small groups of women appeared in the square, trying to join us at the Strangers' Entrance. They carried little banners inscribed with various mottoes. [...] These banners the police seized and tore in pieces. Then they laid hands on the women and literally threw them from one man to another. Some of the police used their fists, striking the women in their faces, their breasts, their shoulders.

One woman I saw thrown down with violence three or four times in rapid succession until at last she lay only half conscious against the curb, and in a serious condition was carried away by kindly strangers. Every moment the struggle grew fiercer, as more and more women arrived on the scene. Women, many of them eminent in art, in medicine and science, women of European reputation, subjected to treatment that would not have been meted out to criminals, and all for the offence of insisting upon the right of peaceful petition.

The struggle lasted for about an hour, more and more women successfully pushing their way past the police and gaining the steps of the House. Then the mounted police were summoned to turn the women back. But, desperately determined, the women, fearing not the hoofs of the horses or the crushing violence of the police, did not swerve from their purpose. [...] For a long time, nearly five hours, the police continued to hustle and beat the women, the crowds becoming more turbulent in their defence. Then, at last the police were obliged to make arrests. One hundred and fifteen women and four men, most of them bruised and choked and otherwise injured, were arrested.

How does Emmeline Pankhurst use language to describe how the protesters were treated? **(12 marks)**

> **Checklist for success**
> - In this response, select no more than four language features.
> - Make sure you give an example of each one.
> - Make a comment that explains what the feature is actually doing.
> - Develop that comment by deciding on what it makes you think of, feel or imagine.

Question 4

For this question, you need to refer to the whole of Source A together with the whole of Source B.

Compare how the writers have conveyed their different views and perspectives on the right to vote.

In your answer, you could:

- compare their views and perspectives on the right to vote
- compare the methods they use to present those ideas and perspectives
- support your ideas with quotations from both texts. **(16 marks)**

Checklist for success

- Understand and explain the key connections between the two texts.
- Use the AO1 S.Q.I. structure (Statement, Quotation, Inference).
- Lead into an AO2 point (Writer's method + example + effect).
- Use the **both/however/whereas** key words to structure your comparison.

Section B: Writing

You are advised to spend 45 minutes on the exam task.

You must write in full sentences.

You are reminded of the need to plan your answer.

You should leave enough time to check your work at the end.

Question 5

'Some young people find politics boring and irrelevant to them; others feel it's important to have their views heard by politicians.'

Write a letter to your MP arguing for the changes you would like to see the government making, for young people now, and in the future.

(24 marks for content and organisation
16 marks for technical accuracy) **(40 marks)**

Checklist for success

A successful response should include:

- a clear sense of your point of view and your reasons for it
- a convincing argument, supported by well-developed ideas
- language style and rhetorical features matched to the task and audience
- a structure that is persuasive and logical.

Check your progress: Section A

Grade 8

- I can summarise and critically evaluate with detailed and perceptive understanding.
- I can understand and respond with insight to explicit and implicit meanings and viewpoints.
- I can analyse and critically evaluate detailed aspects of language, grammar and structure.
- I can back up my understanding and opinions with judicious references and supporting quotations.
- I can make convincing links between texts.

Grade 5

- I can summarise and evaluate with accuracy and clear understanding.
- I can understand and make valid responses to explicit and implicit meanings and viewpoints.
- I can analyse and evaluate relevant aspects of language, grammar and structure.
- I can support my understanding and opinions with sensibly chosen references to texts.
- I can make sensible links between texts.

Grade 2

- I can describe and summarise with some accuracy and understanding.
- I can respond in a straightforward way to most explicit information and viewpoints.
- I can make some relevant comments about language and structure.
- I can support my comments and opinions with some general references.
- I can make straightforward links between texts.

Check your progress: Section B

Grade 8

- I can communicate with impact.
- I can produce an ambitious and effectively structured piece of writing.
- I can use a wide range of well-selected sentence types and structures, and use precise vocabulary for impact.
- I can spell, punctuate and use grammar accurately so that writing is virtually error-free.

Grade 5

- I can communicate effectively and hold my reader's interest.
- I can produce a well-structured and purposeful piece of writing.
- I can vary my sentence types and structures, and use vocabulary for effect.
- I can spell, punctuate and use grammar accurately with occasional errors.

Grade 2

- I can communicate simply in English with some clarity for my reader.
- I can produce writing with a basic structure and some awareness of purpose.
- I can show some control over sentences and use familiar vocabulary.
- I can spell, punctuate and use grammar with a little accuracy.

Glossary of key terms

adverbs: words that modify verbs to describe how something is being done

alliteration: repetition of a sound, usually (but not always) at the start of a sequence of words

anecdotes: mini stories which add weight to the point you are making

audience: the person or people you are writing for; your readership

clause: the basic part of a sentence containing a noun together with a verb, for example, 'The boy ran.'

command: a sentence that tells us to do something by putting the verb first to emphasise the action

complex sentence: develops ideas in a simple sentence and adds detail and information in subsections known as subordinate clauses

compound sentence: when two ideas (which could be simple sentences) are joined together. They are joined with conjunctions such as for, and, nor, but, or, yet, so

conjunctions: joining words or connectives such as for, and, nor, but, or, yet, so

connotations: the associations and connections we make when we think about particular words. For example, the connotations of the word 'red' might include love, passion, danger, fire or heat

conventions: the kinds of features that are often found or associated with a particular form

determiner: a word or phrase which indicates the distance between ideas or things in a text.
For example, 'those books' (far away); 'these books' (close to hand)

direct address: using 'you' or 'your' to make it feel like we have a shared viewpoint or responsibility.

exclamation: a sentence that expresses an emotion such as shock, anger or surprise

explaining: unpicking something for your reader and making it clear; presenting reasons and helping your reader understand something

explicit meaning: the basic information on the surface – the true or literal; what is stated directly

factual: information that is true and can be proved

fiction: any type of story that is from the imagination of its writer

first-person narrator: when a character in a story tells it in their voice using 'I'. This makes it feel like they are sharing their experiences with you

form: category or types of texts that have similar characteristics

hyperbolic questions: exaggerated questions designed to make particular points

implicit meanings: the meanings that you have to work out by reading between the lines; things that are suggested rather than stated

inclusive pronoun: when a writer uses the words 'our' or 'we' to make it feel like we are in a group, and have a shared viewpoint or responsibility. For example: *We must all act now to save our planet.*

infer: conclude by reasoning what you have been able to read between the lines

inference: the explanation of what you have been able to read between the lines

informing: telling your reader about something; presenting them with crisp, clear factual information

listing: a sequence or pattern created by putting words with something in common together, separated by commas. Things are often listed in groups of three for impact

minor sentence: a sentence that lacks one or more of the elements that go to make up a full sentence, for example, a subject or a main verb

modification: changing the impression or image of something by changing the word or words that describe it

monosyllabic: a word that is made up of only one syllable, for example, 'no'

narrative perspective: the point of view from which a story is told

non-fiction: a piece of writing, which is true, factual or about real-life events, for example, newspaper articles, blogs, biographies, autobiographies, letters, diaries, travel writing

novels: long stories with characters and actions, usually organised into chapters or sections

op-ed article: an article or essay in a newspaper, expressing the opinions or viewpoint of a writer who does not work for that newspaper

personification: a type of metaphor where an inanimate object is given human characteristics such as emotions

persuading: getting a reader on your side and sharing your views or attitudes

prefixes: a cluster of letters that can be added to the beginning of a word to create a new one, for example, **un** + happy

pronoun: a word such as I, he, she, we, they or it that replaces a noun in a sentence

purpose: the 'job' your piece of writing is doing, for example, narrating, describing, persuading

register: the choice of vocabulary, grammar and style you make for your audience, for example, formal or informal

rhetorical language features: language techniques designed to persuade a reader to consider an idea from a different point of view

rhetorical questions: questions which are designed to make the reader think, not to answer directly

simile: form of comparison using 'as' or 'like'

simple sentence: presents one idea. It will have one verb or verb phrase and contain one action, event, or state

statement: a sentence that declares something and presents it as a fact or opinion

statistic: when numbers or figures are used in a text as factual evidence

suffixes: a cluster of letters that can be added to the end of a word to create a new one, for example, sad + **ness**

synthesise: draw together information from one or more sources

third-person narrator: when a story is told objectively using 'he', 'she,' 'they'. This can make it feel like an outside observer is telling the story, looking in

tone: links to the idea of 'tone of voice'. It suggests a sound quality or 'voice' in the text that is speaking to you in a particular way

verbs: actions or doing words that are the driving force of the sentence. They can show movement, action, states of being, and can also communicate when things are happening, depending on their tense, for example, past, present, future

Acknowledgements

The publishers gratefully acknowledge the permissions granted to reproduce copyright material in this book. Every effort has been made to contact the holders of copyright material, but if any have been inadvertently overlooked, the Publisher will be pleased to make the necessary arrangements at the first opportunity.

Extract on page 11 from 'The Darkness Out There' in Pack of Cards: Stories 1978–1986, Penelope Lively, 1984 published by Penguin, New Ed (3 Dec. 1987) with permission from David Higham Associates; Extract on pages 15–16 from Your Shoes by Michèle Roberts. Copyright: © Michèle Roberts with permission from Aitken Alexander; Extract on pages 19–20 from Lord of the Flies by William Golding, Faber and Faber Ltd; Extract on pages 26, 27, 29 from The Generation Game by Sophie Duffy, Legend Press (1 Aug. 2011), Legend Press with permission; Extract on page 31 from 'Gazebo' in What we talk about when we talk about love by Raymond Carver published by Vintage (5 Nov. 2009). Reproduced by permission of The Random House Group Ltd; Extract on pages 31–32 from Roof Space by David Grubb in Best British Short Stories 2014 edited by Nicholas Royle reproduced with permission of Salt Publishing via PLSclear; Extract on page 33 from Wish I was here by Jackie Kay Picador (18 April 2007) reproduced with permission of Pan Macmillan via PLSclear; Extract on pages 35–36 from Ladies day by Vicki Jarrett in Best British Short Stories 2014 edited by Nicholas Royle, reproduced with permission of Salt Publishing via PLSclear; Extract on page 38 from Junk by Melvyn Burgess published by Penguin with permission from United Agents; Extract on page 41 from The Girl with the Dragon Tattoo by Stieg Larsson © Norstedts 2008. Reproduced by permission of Quercus Editions Limited; Extract on page 43 from 'Everything Stuck to him' in What we talk about when we talk about love by Raymond Carver published by Vintage (5 Nov. 2009). Reproduced by permission of The Random House Group; Extract on pages 58–60 from Dandelion Wine by Ray Bradbury, published by HarperCollins. Reprinted by permission of HarperCollins Publishers Ltd © Ray Bradbury 2012; Extract on page 61 from The God of Small Things by Arundhati Roy, published by HarperCollins, by Arundhati Roy, copyright © Arundhati Roy, 1997; Extract on pages 72–74, 76–78 © Jon McGregor, If Nobody Speaks of Remarkable Things, Bloomsbury Publishing Plc; Extract on pages 81–82 from The Girl with the Dragon Tattoo by Stieg Larsson © Norstedts 2008. Reproduced by permission of Quercus Editions Limited; Extract on page 104 © Khaled Hosseini, 5 Sept. 2011, The Kite Runner, Bloomsbury Publishing Plc; Extract on pages 110–111 from The Veldt by Ray Bradbury, published by Perfection Learning (21 Nov. 2008) with permission from Don Congdon Associates, Inc; Extract on page 124 from Quora by Michael Santos, MichaelSantos.com; Article on pages 126–128 from Secret Teacher: teaching in prisons is where I can make a real difference, The Guardian, 3 May 2014. Copyright Guardian News & Media Ltd 2016; Extract on page 131 from Race to the Pole by James Cracknel and Ben Fogle Pan, Reprints edition (7 May 2010) published by Pan Macmillan, reproduced with permission of Pan Macmillan via PLSclear; Article on page 142 from My London, and Welcome to it, AA Gill, The New York Times, 27 April, 2012 © 2012 The New York Times. All rights reserved. Used by permission and protected by the Copyright Laws of the United States. The printing, copying, redistribution, or retransmission of this Content without express written permission is prohibited; Article on page 149 from Sleeping rough for charity hides the real homelessness crisis, by Alistair Sloan, 29 Oct 2013. Copyright Guardian News & Media Ltd 2013; Extract on pages 156–157 from The Road to Wigan Pier by George Orwell (Copyright © George Orwell, 1937). Reprinted by permission of Bill Hamilton as the Literary Executor of the Estate of the Late Sonia Brownell Orwell. Copyright © 1958 and renewed 1956 by The Estate of Sonia B. Orwell. Used by permission of Penguin Books Ltd and Houghton Mifflin Harcourt Publishing Company. All Rights Reserved; Extract on pages 160–161 from Jessica Ennis: Unbelievable – From My Childhood Dreams To Winning Olympic Gold, published by Hodder Paperbacks (1 Aug. 2013), Copyright © 2012 Jessica Ennis. Reproduced by Hodder and Stoughton Limited; Extract on pages 168–170 from Looking for Adventure by Steve Backshall Swordfish published by Orion Publishing, with permission from The Orion Publishing Group, London; Article on page 176 from Why I'm taking my child out of school for a holiday, The Guardian, 29 Jan 2014. Copyright Guardian News & Media Ltd 2014; Article on page 178 from Why I'll never take my children out of school for a holiday by Joanna Moorhead The Guardian, 29 Jan 2014. Copyright Guardian News & Media Ltd 2014; Article on page 190 from Cases of modern day slavery are 'on the rise' in Britain by Julie McCaffrey, The Telegraph, 31st Oct 2014, © Telegraph Media Group Limited 2014; Article on pages 196–197 from Why black models are rarely in fashion by Hadley Freeman, The Guardian, 18 Feb 2014. Copyright Guardian News & Media Ltd 2014; Extract on page 200 from How to be a Woman by Caitlin Moran published by Ebury Press (1 Mar. 2012). Reproduced by permission of The Random House Group Ltd; Article on pages 208–209 from In Dismaland, Banksy has created something truly depressing by Jonathan Jones, The Guardian, 21 August 2015. Copyright Guardian News & Media Ltd 2015; Article on pages 212–213 from The Hole in the Wall Project and the Power of Self-Organized Learningl by Sugata Mitra. Originally published 2012 © Edutopia.org; George Lucas Educational Foundation; Article on page 216–217 Leader, 'Ban this barbaric sport', from The Guardian, 18 December 2000. Copyright Guardian News & Media Ltd 2016; Article on pages 223–224 Rio world cup demolitions leave favela families trapped in ghost towns by Tom Phillips, 26 April 2011. Copyright Guardian News & Media Ltd 2011; Article on pages 230–231 Britain's Child soldiers by Michael Bartlet 11 March 2011. Copyright Guardian News & Media Ltd 2011; Article on pages 234–236 The Queen's Diamond Jubilee: I have memories to treasure forever by Gordon Rayner, The Telegraph, 5 June 2012 © Telegraph Media Group Limited 2012; Extract on pages 224–245 from The Electric Michaelangelo by Sarah Hall, Faber and Faber Ltd; Article on pages 250–251 from Why don't young people vote, The Huffington Post, Nov 12 2015, with permission from Hanan Esaili.

The publishers would like to thank the following for permission to use reproduce pictures in these pages:

Cover images © Everett Historical/Shutterstock, © MissionMike/Shutterstock

p8: Everett Historical/Shutterstock, p10: David J. Green/Alamy, p11: Andreas von Einsiedel/Alamy, p14: Laborant/Shutterstock, p16: Gary Roebuck/Alamy, p18: Roberto Herrett/Alamy, p20: AF archive/Alamy, p22: magicmomentsbymarianne/Shutterstock, p27: redsnapper/Alamy, p29: Ljupco Smokovski/Shutterstock, p31: KieferPix/Shutterstock, p33: Bikeriderlondon/Shutterstock, p35: ALAN EDWARDS/Alamy, p37: ADRIAN DENNIS/ AFP/Getty Images, p38: Anna Bizon/Getty Images, p45: Daniel Fung/Shutterstock, p46, 49: Artepics/Alamy, p48: Wlad74/Shutterstock, p50: MissionMike/Shutterstock, p52: Pavelk/Shutterstock, p57l: Nicram Sabod/Shutterstock, p57r: Scorpp/Shutterstock, p60: Snowturtle/Shutterstock, p62: Anuj Nair/Moment Open/Getty Images, p65: Semmick Photo/Shutterstock, p67: Stone36/Shutterstock, p68: Michael Lloyd/EyeEm/Getty Images, p70tl: Mubus7/ Shutterstock, p70tr: Kevin Eaves/Shutterstock, p70bl: Helen Hotson/Shutterstock, p70br: Www.dennisoswald.de/ Getty Images, p73: Planet News Archive/Getty Images, p76: Tithi Luadthong/Shutterstock, p79: Matyas Rehak/ Shutterstock, p82: Wataru Yanagida/Getty Images, p85: Moviestore collection Ltd/Alamy, p87: Peter Adams Photography Ltd/Alamy, p89: stocker1970/Shutterstock, p90-91: Mike Pellinni/Shutterstock, p93: Tuul and Bruno Morandi/Getty Images, p95: IMG Imagery/Shutterstock, p96-87: estherpoon/Shutterstock, p98: fivepointsix/ Shutterstock, p100-101: VanderWolf Images/Shutterstock, p103: REUTERS /Alamy, p105: AF archive/Alamy, p107-108: Nate Derrick/Shutterstock, p110: Microstocker1/Shutterstock, p112: Nejron Photo/Shutterstock, p115: Photos 12/Alamy, p117: Photos 12/Alamy, p120: b-hide the scene/Shutterstock, p125: Halfdark/Getty Images, p126: Sergio Azenha/Alamy, p127: Mark Harvey/Alamy, p128-129: Paul J Martin/Shutterstock, p133: Popperfoto/Getty Images, p136: DEA PICTURE LIBRARY/Getty Images, p141: Walker Art Library/Alamy, p142: Bikeworldtravel/Shutterstock, p144-145: Mary Evans Picture Library/Alamy, p147: Mikadun/Shutterstock, p149: Paul Bradbury/Getty Images, p150: Heritage Images/Getty Images, p152: Tony Baggett/Shutterstock, p155: ANDREW HOLBROOKE/Corbis/Getty Images, p156: Bentley Archive/Popperfoto/Getty Images, p159: Mary Evans Picture Library/TOWN & COUNTRY PLANNING, p161: John Maclean/Getty Images, p163: Aflo Co. Ltd./Alamy, p164: Hulton Archive/Getty Images, p166: CORBIS/Getty Images, p169: Janelle Lugge/Shutterstock, p170: WENN Ltd / Alamy, p172-173: Mary Evans Picture Library/Alamy, p177: Monkey Business Images/Shutterstock, p181: Dasha Petrenko/Shutterstock, p184: Cem Ozdel/Anadolu Agency/Getty Images, p186: Scott J. Ferrell/Congressional Quarterly/Getty Images, p189: DEA PICTURE LIBRARY/Getty Images, p190: OJPHOTOS/Alamy, p192: Getty Images, p195: Hadrian/Shutterstock, p197: Joe Kohen/Getty Images, p198: Victor VIRGILE/Getty Images, p200: Mireya Acierto/Getty Images, p202-203: Adisa/Shutterstock, p204: Versta/Shutterstock, p207: Matthias Tunger/Getty Images, p208: Matthew Baker/ Getty Images, p212: Pixelfusion3d/Getty Images, p214: Hulton Archive/Getty Images, p217: Herb Scharfman/ Sports Imagery/Getty Images, p220: Comstock Images/Stockbyte/Getty Images, p223: Donatas Dabravolskas/ Shutterstock, p227: Stephen Dorey/Alamy, p229: Granger Historical Picture Archive/Alamy, p230: Marc Charuel/ Getty Images, p235: Samir Hussein/WireImage/Getty Images, p247: Grachev Alexey/Shutterstock